The clarity of style for which Mr. Brooks has long been noted is displayed to advantage in this newest book of his criticism. Originally delivered as lectures at a faculty conference of people interested in theology, the critical studies have special importance for all readers who would like a fresh perspective on five distinguished literary figures whose Christian commitment has been regarded as nonexistent or nebulous.

Mr. Brooks believes that whatever a writer has to say about mankind, Christianity, or culture in general is most significantly explained through his achievements as an artist, and for that reason the critic here deals with the characteristic literary work of each author, rather than with his theology or philosophy.

Cleanth Brooks is Gray Professor of Rhetoric at Yale University.

"The commentary has a remarkable freshness and clarity . . . there are not many other books of the last few years so perfectly calculated as his to communicate to the general reader some sense of the exhilaration that is to be gained from the modern literary imagination at its best."

THE HIDDEN GOD

THE HIDDEN GOD

Studies in Hemingway, Faulkner, Yeats, Eliot, and Warren

By CLEANTH BROOKS

NEW HAVEN AND LONDON, YALE UNIVERSITY PRESS

Third printing, February 1964.
Designed by Crimilda Pontes,
set in Monotype Aldine Bembo type.
Printed in the United States of America by
The Carl Purington Rollins Printing-Office
of the Yale University Press.

Library of Congress catalog card number: 63–9308

In memoriam patris qui cum libros
me docuit amare tum librum librorum.

". . . every religion which does not affirm that God is hidden is not true. . . . Vere tu es Deus absconditus."

Pascal, *Pensées*

PREFACE

The five lectures included in this book represent substantially those that I gave in June 1955 at the Conference in Theology for College Faculty, held at Trinity College, Hartford. During the past year, I have completely rewritten the second and fifth lectures. This circumstance will account for the mention in the lecture on R. P. Warren of poetry and fiction published by him as recently as 1961. In rewriting the lecture, it seemed pointless to limit my discussion to work that was in print in 1955. In preparing this little book for publication, however, I have tried in general to preserve the quality of spoken utterance. These discussions were originally conceived as lectures and are here frankly presented as such.

I have quite deliberately included writers whose views of reality are not orthodox and may not even be Christian. It would not have been difficult to find other writers besides T. S. Eliot who are active churchmen and whose Christian position is a matter of record. But I thought it would be more useful to the audience for which these lectures were originally designed if I ranged more widely and dealt with some of the more interesting, if problematic, cases—cases sometimes the more interesting because problematic. But if the orthodoxy or even the minimal Christianity of any of my five authors is in question, there can be no question about his significance as an artist. For these writers, though they represent different literary generations, are, it would be generally agreed, among the best that our twentieth-century English-speaking world has produced. Their insights into the nature of that world are bound to be of moment to every reader, whether he be Christian or non-Christian or simply a seeker after truth.

In addition to their original presentation, these lectures have been given as a series at Notre Dame University and Earlham College, and some of them have been given as single lectures at Syracuse University, Dartmouth College, Drew University, Boston College, the Yale Divinity School, Rockhurst College, the College English Association of New England, Clark University, and the Louisiana State University, at New Orleans and at Baton Rouge. The second lecture has appeared in *The Massachusetts Review*; portions of the fifth lecture, in *The Centenary Review* and *The Georgia Review*. Grateful acknowledgment is made to the editors of these magazines for permission to reprint the material here.

I have a special acknowledgment to make to Professor W. Norman Pittenger of the General Theological Seminary, who has kindly read the lectures in manuscript and has made suggestions that I have been happy to incorporate in my text.

Grateful acknowledgment also is made to the following for permission to use quotations:
Charles Scribner's Sons, Jonathan Cape, Ltd., and the executors of the Ernest Hemingway estate for excerpts from Hemingway's "A Clean, Well-Lighted Place" (copyright 1933, Charles Scribner's Sons, copyright © 1961, Ernest Hemingway); "In Another Country" (copyright 1927, Charles Scribner's Sons,

copyright © 1955, Ernest Hemingway); *For Whom the Bell Tolls* (copyright 1940, Ernest Hemingway); *The Sun Also Rises* (copyright 1926, Charles Scribner's Sons, copyright © 1954, Ernest Hemingway).

Random House, Inc., for excerpts from Faulkner's *Sanctuary* (copyright 1931, © 1958, William Faulkner); *The Sound and the Fury* (copyright 1929, 1930, William Faulkner); *Absalom, Absalom!* (copyright 1936, William Faulkner); *The Unvanquished* (copyright 1935, 1938, William Faulkner); *Light in August* (copyright 1932, William Faulkner).

The Macmillan Company, A. P. Watt and Son, and Mrs. W. B. Yeats for excerpts from Yeats' *Collected Poems* (copyright 1906, 1912, 1916, 1919, 1924, 1928, 1933, The Macmillan Company, copyright 1940, 1944, 1946, 1952, 1956, 1961, Bertha Georgie Yeats); *Autobiography* (copyright 1916, The Macmillan Company, copyright 1944, Bertha Georgie Yeats); *A Vision* (copyright 1938, The Macmillan Company); *The Letters of W. B. Yeats* by Allen Wade (copyright 1953, 1954, Anne Butler Yeats).

Harcourt, Brace & World, Inc., and Faber and Faber, Ltd., for excerpts from Eliot's *Murder in the Cathedral* (copyright 1935, Harcourt, Brace & World, Inc.); *The Cocktail Party* (copyright 1950, T. S. Eliot); *Four Quartets* (copyright 1943, T. S. Eliot); *Collected Poems 1901–1935* (copyright 1936, Harcourt, Brace & World, Inc.); *The Rock* (copyright 1934, Harcourt, Brace & World, Inc., copyright © 1962, T. S. Eliot); *The Family Reunion* (copyright 1939, T. S. Eliot). Harvard University Press and Faber and Faber, Ltd., for excerpts from Eliot's *The Use of Poetry* (copyright 1933, The President and Fellows of Harvard College).

Random House, Inc., and Eyre & Spottiswoode, Ltd., for excerpts from Warren's *Brother to Dragons* (copyright 1953,

Robert Penn Warren); *Promises* (copyright © 1955, 1957, Robert Penn Warren); *Wilderness* (copyright © 1961, Robert Penn Warren). Random House, Inc., for excerpts from Warren's *You, Emperors and Others* (copyright © 1958, 1959, 1960, Robert Penn Warren). The William Morris Agency for excerpts from Warren's *Selected Poems 1923–1943* (copyright 1944, Robert Penn Warren). Harcourt, Brace & World, Inc., for excerpts from Warren's *All the King's Men* (copyright 1946, Harcourt, Brace & World, Inc.).

New Haven, Connecticut
July 1962

C.B.

CONTENTS

THE STATE OF MODERN LITERATURE

A PRELIMINARY NOTE

When the solid citizen of our time looks at modern literature—if he looks at it at all—he usually finds much to deplore. When a newspaper pundit like J. Donald Adams of the New York *Times* has looked at it, he has on occasion broken down into grumpy scolding. When *Time* magazine looks at it, it finds it gravely deficient for American morale-building. When the average liberal intellectual looks at it, he does find some things of which to approve—the honesty, the attacks on racism, the increasing comprehension of the dignity of the individual even among the poor and oppressed—but he also finds many of our best writers defective in their sympathies and hopelessly old-fashioned in their prejudices: T. S. Eliot is wedded to obscurantism; W. B. Yeats, great poet that he was, at one time flirted dangerously with Fascism; William Faulkner could never really qualify for membership in Americans for Democratic Action. But a Christian looking at modern literature ought to find a great deal that is heartening and hopeful.

Our modern literature represents a great achievement—the

more triumphant because it has been made under the very worst of conditions, and therefore testifies to real vitality. My more approving estimate of the situation calls for some qualifications and explanations. In the first place, I draw a careful distinction between the machine-made popular arts of our time and the work of our serious artists. An industrial civilization has undertaken the mass production of entertainment to fill up the leisure which it has created. And whereas there is much to be said for the mass production of refrigerators or automobiles, there is very little to be said for the mass production of art. The genuine artist presumably undertakes to set forth some vision of life—some imaginative apprehension of it which he hopes will engage our imagination. He gives us his own intuition—his own insight into the human situation. It may prove to be a paltry insight; it may constitute a trivial view; but it is at least one which the artist has had the faith to explore and to test by attempting to objectify it for us. But the worker on the mass-production line that is turning out prefabricated entertainment starts from a radically different assumption: he gives nothing and means to give nothing. Rather, he hopes to play upon the stock emotions and stereotyped attitudes already present in the minds of his audience, releasing them by applying the proper stimulus, giving the reader or the auditor the illusion of something new but actually making sure that he never departs from the limits of the sure-fire stereotypes.

In view of the situation, we have no right to expect that such art will be more than a time-killer or perhaps a pain-killer, a mild narcotic. But narcotics provide no nourishment, and constant indulgence in them can numb and deaden the faculties of apprehension. I am convinced that a deadening of the imagination has occurred. William Wordsworth in 1800 claimed that the imagination was being strangled by the more sensational popular arts, though few people, I think, then took, or now take, seriously his analysis of the situation. I take it very seriously. I think that nineteenth-century literature bears the mark of serious injury occasioned by precisely the forces that he described. Be that as it may, the pressure of the popular arts today as exerted through cheap fiction, Tin Pan Alley, the movies, the radio, and now television makes what Wordsworth faced in 1800 seem very mild indeed.

I do not intend to enlarge on the damage done by the powerful and continuous impact of cheap art—*kitsch*. But in talking about contemporary literature, I feel obliged to indicate that I am taking it into account. After all, for more than half of our citizens it is the only contemporary literature that exists. Furthermore, the tremendous chasm that exists between our best literature and our popular literature is itself one of the most significant phenomena of our present cultural situation. And let no one protest that we have always had shoddy art alongside the great art of the age. That is true enough. There has always been hill and dale, mountain and plain. But the present situation gives us the towering height of the Andes separated by only a relatively few miles from the depths of the Atacama Trench of the South Pacific; and if I may press the geological analogy a little further, great height and great depth so narrowly separated always signify a critical imbalance—a pattern of stresses and strains that portends earthquakes and violent convulsions of the earth's crust.

Lastly, and principally, I have called attention to the all-pervading pressure of contemporary popular art because of its effect upon our ability to recognize and respond to the genuine literature of our day. We confuse a William Faulkner with a Tennessee Williams, for do they not both emphasize sex and violence? We can see no real difference between a novel by Robert Penn Warren and one by Frank Yerby or Mrs. Keyes, for all of them are historical novels, aren't they? Or, having become so habituated to *kitsch* that we have forgotten what the true nature of art is, we conclude that the only thing really wrong with popular art is that it has no serious message, and so we demand that our serious writers begin to insert serious messages, plainly labeled as such and calculated to sell the idea in question to the wayfaring reader. That is, we tend to confuse poetics with poetical rhetoric; we talk of literature as if it were a pure work of the will, not an effect of the imagination; and in our modern mythology the muse becomes not a willful and capricious goddess who bestows her favors unpredictably and as an act of grace but the neat and efficient rewrite girl in a high-powered advertising office, who may occasionally make a bright suggestion and who can be counted upon to work up the specific job assigned.

This is why some newspaper pundits are perpetually scolding the modern poet for being a willful obscurantist. This is why some professors and editors, alarmed at the state of the nation, can with straight faces request the production of a novel that will strengthen American morale. This is why so many people, including some of our brighter liberal critics, persist in demanding an "affirmative" literature—as if any true work of the imagination were not already affirmative in the only sense in which we can ask it to be. The only really negative literature that I know of is bad or defective literature. I suspect, further, that the only affirmative literature that will actually satisfy the quarters most vocal in demanding it is a literature that finally argues for the passage of a particular bill or for the election of a specific political party.

In any case, it is for something else that one looks when he comes to estimate the achievement of the serious writers of our times—something more inward than a tract—something deeper and more resonant than a tirade against a particular abuse. One looks for an image of man, attempting in a world increasingly dehumanized to realize himself as a man—to act like a responsible moral being, not to drift like a mere thing.

All that I have said bears very directly, of course, upon the problem of Christian literature. We have today many able writers who are specifically and committedly Christian, but some of our literature that is most significant for the Christian reader has been written by authors who are not members of any church and by some who frankly put themselves down as agnostics or atheists. If we demand of our serious literature that it make overt preachments of Christianity, we shall certainly exclude some of the most spiritually nourishing literature of our time. But I shall press this warning further still. If we read such Christian writers as T. S. Eliot or W. H. Auden merely for the sake of the overt preachments that their works may be felt to make, we shall probably miss their significance as Christian artists. For if we cannot apprehend their art, we have lost the element that makes their work significant to us; they might as well be journalists or pamphleteers.

2.

ERNEST HEMINGWAY

MAN ON HIS MORAL UPPERS

It is in a general context of the sort described in the preceding note that I wish to discuss the work of Ernest Hemingway. Hemingway is a writer who, through most of his mature life, seems to have had no religious commitment. Indeed, his work is regarded by some people as hostile to religion and perhaps as subversive to Christian morals. (I am aware that Mr. Carlos Baker in his book on Hemingway published a few years ago averred that the Book of Common Prayer was seldom out of Hemingway's reach. Mr. Baker may have been familiar with the appointments of Hemingway's writing desk and therefore have known specifically whereof he spoke. But I wonder whether Hemingway's closeness to the Prayer Book could be inferred from Hemingway's fiction.) I am not, therefore, relying upon a presumed Christianity when I say that the Christian reader may derive something very important from Hemingway's work. For Hemingway at his best depicts brilliantly the struggle of man to be a human being in a world which increasingly seeks to reduce him to a mechanism, a mere thing.

One of the best introductions to Hemingway that I know occurs in a piece of writing that never mentions him by name. Paul Tillich, in a section of his book *Theology of Culture*, discusses "the special character of contemporary culture." He sees the predominant movement of our culture as the spirit of industrial society, but he also finds an increasingly powerful protest against the spirit of industrialism. Under industrialism, man has made a progressive conquest of nature, both outside and inside himself. But though this conquest of nature would seem to prove that man was the master of his world and of himself, on the contrary "he has become a part of the reality he has created, an object among objects, a thing among things, a cog within a universal machine to which he must adapt himself in order not to be smashed by it. But this adaptation makes him a means for ends which are means themselves, and in which an ultimate end is lacking. Out of this predicament of man in the industrial society the experiences of emptiness and meaninglessness, of dehumanization and estrangement have resulted."

Tillich goes on to say that our contemporary arts everywhere "show in their style both the encounter with non-being, and the strength which can stand this encounter and shape it creatively." The crucial fight, then, as Tillich sees it, is to save the humanity of man as man. That fight is plainly evident in Hemingway and in modern literature generally. It is the implicit subject of much of our modern poetry and much of our fiction; and what lends particular desperation to the fight, I repeat, is that the serious writer must overturn habits continually built up and fortified by an infected art and that he must try to present his imaginative vision to a reader who is increasingly becoming a thing—a mechanism of conditioned reflexes, an object for calculated manipulation by the advertising man, by the pulp fictioneer, and even by the Book-of-the-Month Club.

We can hardly understand modern literature without reference to these pressures and the resistances to them that have to assert themselves if we are to have a genuine literature at all. Fortunately and significantly, the resistances are there; there is a healthy vitality. Ernest Hemingway would represent perhaps the most simple and elementary instance of this healthy resistance.

Hemingway may be said to portray man on his moral uppers. The Hemingway hero finds in the universe no sanctions for goodness; he sees through what are for him the great lying abstract words, like *glory*, *patriotism*, and *honor*; he has found that the institutions that pretend to foster and safeguard the traditional moral codes are bankrupt. But in a hostile universe—or in what is at the least an indifferent and meaningless universe—the Hemingway hero clings to a lonely virtue. If his virtue is an elemental virtue like courage, and if it is exercised as an effect of almost quixotic pride, still it is virtue, and he who exercises it thereby defines himself as a man, and repudiates mere thinghood. The Italian major in the story "In Another Country" says that he does not believe in bravery, but unwittingly he gives a lesson in bravery, or perhaps it is a lesson in something better than bravery. The old bull-fighter in "The Undefeated" is finally defeated, but only on his own terms. So it is in every one of Hemingway's successful stories.

An excellent example of Hemingway's basic theme is furnished by the fine but very brief story "A Clean, Well-Lighted Place." The plot is so simple as to seem nonexistent. Two waiters in a cafe, late at night, talk about an old man who comes there to drink brandy. The old man has tried to commit suicide, and they speculate on the reasons for his despair. Finally they put him out, close up the cafe, and prepare to go home. The story ends with the speculations of the older waiter. Just before he tells the younger waiter good night he confesses that each night he is "reluctant to close up because there may be someone who needs the cafe." When the younger waiter retorts that "there are bodegas open all night long," the older waiter tries to explain what he means by the need for the cafe. A cafe like the one in which they work is well-lighted. It is a clean and pleasant place, and "now, there are shadows on the leaves." But, after the younger waiter has gone his way, the older man's mind continues to play over the problem and he tries to discover just what it is that the cafe provides for people like the old man, and—as it becomes clear—for people like himself.

He turns off the light, but as he leaves the cafe, he continues "the conversation with himself." The place has to be orderly, clean, pleasant, and well-lighted. Music is not necessary. He, for one, doesn't want it. A bar is not at all a substitute. Why? Because you cannot "stand before a bar with dignity although that is all that is provided for these hours." Abruptly, he puts the question to himself: what do I fear? Actually the emotion is not fear or dread. It was "a nothing." It was "all a nothing and a man was nothing too. It was only that and light was all it needed and a certain cleanness and order. Some lived in it and never felt it but he knew it all was nada y pues nada y nada y pues nada. Our nada who art in nada," and the older waiter goes on to the end with his somber parody of the Lord's Prayer.

As he walks on, he passes a bar, and stops to order a cup or coffee, and while the coffee is being poured, he comments, since his mind is still occupied with cafes as refuges from the dark, that the light here is present but that the bar needs polishing. The barman is too tired to take umbrage or even to talk at all. He simply asks whether the waiter wants more coffee. He doesn't. He wants something else which he knows he will not get, and so starts his walk home.

"He disliked bars and bodegas. A clean, well-lighted cafe was a very different thing. Now, without thinking further, he would go home to his room. He would lie in the bed and finally, with daylight, he would go to sleep. After all, he said to himself, it is probably only insomnia. Many must have it."

I am doing violence to a remarkably brilliant and deft story in paraphrasing it and in quoting only a few fragments from the last pages. What one really ought to do at this point is to read the story in its entirety, for it summarizes brilliantly Hemingway's basic moral preoccupation. Man finds himself in a meaningless universe. The best that he can hope to do is to find some little area of order which he himself has made within the engulfing dark of the ultimate nothing. He wants to sit in a place which is orderly and tidy—the bar must be clean, and it must be lighted—and there, sipping his brandy, he is able, perhaps, to confront with some dignity the invading disorder and even stare it down. But the order and the light are supplied by *him*. They do *not* reflect an inherent, though concealed, order in the universe. What little meaning there is in the world is imposed upon that world by man. Once we realize this, we shall have no difficulty in understanding why Hemingway appeals so powerfully to the French Existentialists. Indeed I should assign to Hemingway the same role that Professor Tillich assigns to the Existentialists: like the Christian, the Existentialist protests against the dehumanization of man and asserts almost desperately man's dignity as a being capable of moral choice.

"A Clean, Well-Lighted Place" epitomizes Hemingway's conception of man's plight in an alien universe. But this admirable little story is lyric rather than dramatic, and it emphasizes man's capacity for suffering rather than for action as we usually understand the term. One ought therefore to deal more specifically with the situation of the man of action as Hemingway typically treats it. The Hemingway hero, I have said, is doomed to defeat, but he insists upon being defeated on his own terms. There is the matter of the point of honor. For a final success is impossible—it is as a quixotic gesture that the hero makes his choice of acting one way rather than another. It is a mere gesture but it has its importance in that it proclaims him to be a man and not a mere automaton. This insistence upon a code of honor is made by the man of action in dozens of Hemingway stories.

Probably two illustrations of the point will be sufficient. In a story I have already mentioned, "In Another Country," we see those things which make life precious for the Italian major stripped from him. The major has been the best fencer in Italy, but the wound that he has received in the war has shriveled his right hand; and though the doctor assures him that the new treatment will restore the hand to use, it is plain to him (and to us) that he will never fence again. This is the situation as the story opens. What we are allowed to see happen before our eyes is the way in which he receives the loss of his young wife—who dies, during the course of the story suddenly and rather unexpectedly, of pneumonia.

We see the major through the eyes of a young American who has been wounded on the Italian front while serving with the Italian army. The major impresses him as a rather hard little man with a wry sense of humor who does not believe in bravery nor in the new medical theory, and who passes the, to his mind, futile hours in the hospital by trying to teach the young American Italian grammar. But one day to the American boy's surprise, the major suddenly seems to explode in bitterness. They have been speaking casually enough until they get on to the subject of marriage. The major asks the boy what he will do when the war is over.

"Speak grammatically!" he cautions him. When the boy replies that he will go to the States, the major asks whether he is married, to which the young American answers that he hopes soon to be. Suddenly the major rips out:

"The more of a fool you are. A man must not marry."

The boy is puzzled at this explosion and tries to find out why the major believes that a man must not marry.

"'He cannot marry. He cannot marry,' [the major] said angrily. 'If he is to lose everything, he should not place himself in a position to lose that. He should not place himself in a position to lose. He should find things he cannot lose. . . .'

"'But why should he necessarily lose it?'

"'He'll lose it,' the major said. He was looking at the wall. Then he looked down at the machine and jerked his little hand out from between the straps and slapped it hard against his thigh. 'He'll lose it,' he almost shouted. 'Don't argue with me!' Then he called to the attendant who ran the machines. 'Come and turn this damned thing off.'"

But a little later, after his outburst, the major returns to apologize to his young friend. He had not meant to be rude, but he has been under great tension. His wife has been gravely ill with pneumonia; he has now just learned by telephone that his wife has died, and the major suddenly bursts into tears. "I am utterly unable to resign myself," he says.

As the major fights back his tears, straight and soldierly, the American boy suddenly learns that bravery has a dimension that he had not known existed. Three days later the major is back at the hospital, wearing a black mourning band on the sleeve of his uniform, taking the useless treatment for his injured hand, and looking out of the window. The iron reserve—the passionately strict discipline over his feelings—has reasserted itself. There will be no more outbursts from now on, but the American boy has learned something—that an iron reserve can conceal the deepest passion and that there is a kind of stoic endurance far on the other side of bravery.

Yet in this story, I must admit, we are still dealing with an action which is really suffering, and we are here also involved with what is almost a romantic theme—the suffering over the death of a loved one of a man of fine sensibility. For the sake of variety and scope, our second illustration ought therefore to have to do with a course of action deliberately chosen and sustained, and it should have to do, again for contrast, with a more grimy and rough-hewn character. Hemingway's story of the boxing ring, "Fifty Grand," will admirably serve on both counts.

The hero in this story is the aging heavyweight champion who is having difficulty getting in shape for the championship fight and who, finally aware that he is certain to lose the fight, decides to fix the fight and to bet against himself. He is going to lose his title anyway, but by betting against himself he will at least realize some profit out of the end of his boxing career. It is a sordid sellout, to be sure, even though Hemingway has made it plain that the boxer is a good home man who loves his wife and children and who is primarily anxious to provide for them. But a sellout it is, and the fact that we accept it as such will in no wise interfere with our apprehension of the artistic merit of the story.

The gamblers, however, have given the double cross a further twist; they have actually arranged to have the challenger lose by fouling the champion. During the bout, therefore, the boxer suddenly finds himself utterly torn apart by a low blow in the groin, physically sickened with the pain and sick too with the stunning realization that his fortune—he had bet heavily against himself—has in an instant vanished. But the plan of action forms immediately in his pain-numbed mind, and with an almost superhuman courage he holds himself together long enough to carry it out. He is able to summon a sick smile to his face as he assures the referee that he has not really been hurt, that the low blow directed by the challenger was purely accidental, and that the fight should be allowed to go on. He actually manages to convince the referee; the fight does go on, and goes on long enough for him to launch a low blow himself, a blow which fouls his opponent so thoroughly and so cripplingly that the fight is over and his own defeat assured.

On one level the story is certainly sordid enough, but we miss the point completely if we fail to take account of the real heroism displayed. The boxer is courageous, he carries out his plan, he bears up for the necessary time under a pain that is all but intolerable and unmanning. What is in question is not the purity of the boxer in any conventional sense. The immorality on one level has to be conceded: the world in which the boxer lives is depicted with merciless realism. But the nature of that world cannot impugn the sheer heroism that the battered old champion displays as he transcends its shabby crookedness. "Fifty Grand," then, presents Hemingway's basic theme quite as well as Hemingway's *The Old Man and the Sea.* In both stories the dignity of man is asserted and is essential, I believe, at exactly the same moral level. That the one story stinks of the boxing ring and the other is filled with the purifying salt tang of the deep sea does not alter significantly the essential theme.

I do not mean to play down Hemingway's last great success, but I think it would be unjust to the earlier Hemingway to imply that his account of the world was merely negative. Nor do I think that Hemingway in his most recent story now finds the world any more meaningful than he once found it. Hemingway's is a harsh and austere world. But there is never any doubt that in that world a man, a real man, is more than an automaton, a mere thing.

So important for Hemingway is courage that it seems to underlie all the other virtues, as perhaps indeed it does. An article by Maude Royden published in the *Atlantic Monthly* a number of years ago makes this point very convincingly. If one turns the other cheek because he is afraid not to turn it, he is not exhibiting Christianity. That would be Nietzsche's slave morality indeed. The specifically Christian virtue is exercised only by the man who turns his cheek though he is not in the least afraid. Hemingway's emphasis upon courage—and later I shall associate Faulkner's name with this same emphasis—is, as a matter of fact, significant and perhaps necessary as a first step in moving back toward the Christian virtues. Hemingway, of course, stops short of the domain of Christianity proper, but he does see that the man who lacks courage, a mere slave to his fears, is not truly free and not truly human. The point is made over and over again in the stories. It is made perhaps most sharply in an admirable long story entitled "The Short and Happy Life of Francis Macomber."

Macomber "lives" for perhaps something less than an hour, but it is a happy life and as the story implies it is the only real life that he has had. Francis Macomber, though he has gone to the good schools and has a fashionable wife and an excellent income, has never really come into a state of full manhood. He has never grown up. He is a slave to his beautiful and cruel wife, who is openly and contemptuously unfaithful to him. On the African hunting trip with which the story deals, Macomber, after wouning a lion, is afraid to go into the bush to finish him off. He is finally shamed into doing so by the professional hunter and guide; but when the lion shows himself, Francis ignominiously turns tail and runs. That night his wife seeks the bed of the professional hunter and casually admits to the husband what she has done.

But on the next day, while they are hunting buffalo, something happens to Macomber. He suddenly finds that he is not afraid—that he is actually enjoying the excitement and even the danger. Hemingway has managed very cleverly the motivation of this change in Macomber. I find it convincing in spite of its suddenness. But it *is* sudden; it amounts to a conversion. It shocks the incredulous wife and it dazzles and puzzles Macomber himself. Macomber's new life—his first real life—lasts, as I have said, something less than an hour, for an accidental shot blows his brains out. But the implication is perfectly clear. Hemingway could not have made it clearer had he quoted the eighteenth-century poem which boasts that "One crowded hour of glorious life / Is worth an age without a name." Macomber's crowded hour of life justifies, and in some sense compensates for, the long years of slavery in which he was miserable and unhappy because not a real man.

Something like the same theme dominates Hemingway's best known and perhaps finest novel, *For Whom the Bell Tolls*. In this novel of the Spanish Civil War an American, Robert Jordan, argues to himself that the value of a lifetime can be conceivably crowded into the space of two or three days. On a particular mission to destroy a bridge back in the hills he has met the girl Maria, and finds himself powerfully and meaningfully in love. In the desperation of his love for her, Jordan argues to himself that "You have it *now* and that is all your whole life is; now. There is nothing else than now. There is neither yesterday, certainly, nor is there any tomorrow. How old must you be before you know that? There is only now, and if now is only two days, then two days is your life and everything in it will be in proportion. This is how you live a life in two days. And if you stop complaining and asking for what you never will get, you will have a good life. A good life is not measured by any biblical span."

Later, with the mission accomplished, the bridge destroyed, Jordan, badly wounded and unable to escape with Maria and the rest of the party, remains behind to hold up the Fascist advance and give his friends more time for their escape. Lying there with his submachine gun beside him, waiting for the first Fascist rider to come into target range, Jordan tells himself:

"It does no good to think about Maria. Try to believe what you told her. That is the best. And who says it is not true? Not you. You don't say it, any more than you would say the things did not happen that happened. Stay with what you believe now. Don't get cynical. The time is too short and you have just sent her away. Each one does what he can. You can do nothing for yourself but perhaps you can do something for another. Well, we had all our luck in four days. Not four days. It was afternoon when I first got there and it will not be noon today. That makes not quite three days and three nights. Keep it accurate, he said. Quite accurate."

Robert Jordan tells himself at this point that he must get down and turn so that he can fire the machine gun. It is time to make himself useful "instead of leaning against the tree like a tramp." As he continues to talk to himself, he reasons with himself that what is happening is certainly not the worst of things. Indeed he is a very lucky man that the shell which wounded him crushed the nerve in his leg so that below the break he can feel nothing. It is as numb as if it were not part of his body.

He tells himself too that there is no need to be afraid of death. Everyone has to go through it, and once you know you have to, you are no longer afraid of it. But he puts it as a question to himself: "'You are not afraid of it. . . . Are you? No,' he said, 'truly.'"

But Jordan is too honest to try to make the departure from the world less than a painful business. As he looks down the hill slope, he thinks to himself that he hates to leave it all very much. He hopes that he has done some good in the world and he tells himself that he has tried to do some good "with what talent I had." But to say "I had" is to speak as if he were already a dead man, and Jordan means to remain alive to the very last gasp. Besides, he has one more task to do. So he speedily corrects "had" to "have," continuing the dialogue with himself: "*Have, you mean. All right, have.*"

"I have fought for what I believed in for a year now. If we win here we will win everywhere. The world is a fine place and worth the fighting for and I hate very much to leave it. And you had a lot of luck, he told himself, to have had such a good life. You've had just as good a life as grandfather's though not as long. You've had as good a life as any one because of these last days. You do not want to complain when you have been so lucky."

Ernest Hemingway is too thoroughly committed to naturalism and too honest a man to try to delude himself into thinking that one can ever get outside the dimension of time; yet he is aware of what other men have meant in saying that an experience of completeness, wholeness, and power and delight may convey an aspect of eternity. He has probably not read St. Augustine on the subject, and yet his character, the young American Spanish teacher Robert Jordan, might have read St. Augustine, for he tries humbly, clumsily, very honestly, without recourse to mysticism, to say that duration of time does not make a satisfactory life but that a satisfactory life is made rather by a complete satisfaction of the spirit.

One is tempted to find further approximations to Christianity in this novel and particularly in the end of it. Jordan, for example, in telling Maria good-by, reminds her that she must now live for both of them. "Thou art me too now. Thou art all there will be of me," he tells her. The human spirit still craves its immortality. In his trying to tell her that she must now live for both of them, that the only wisp of immortality that he can have will be what remains of him in her mind, there is the touching though finally desperate effort to secularize the conception of immortality and bring it down to some naturalistic possibility. For Jordan is not a supernaturalist. He is a naturalist in all the senses, including his tremendous sensitivity to the realm of nature. He dies as he has lived, loving the feel, smell, and quality of the earth. "He touched the palm of his hand against the pine needles where he lay and he touched the bark of the pine trunk that he lay behind." These are the certainties of the Hemingway world—the intense vibrations of the senses.

Whether or not Jordan keeps his grip on consciousness long enough to cut down the first Fascist horseman will not make very much difference. Maria and her party have already got a good start. Yet Jordan manfully fights off the pain and out of a kind of pride keeps a grip upon himself. He means to die in a certain way in order to go out of life into the nothing with a proper gesture—the proper dignity. It is this that ultimately sustains him to the end—not any practical consideration, not any illusion that he will accomplish anything further of importance for the Loyalist cause, not even any feeling that his action will accomplish anything for Maria.

At this point it is worth reviewing the various attempts which have been made to find in Hemingway some affirmative position. Critics welcomed Hemingway's worst novel, *To Have and to Have Not* when it appeared, because they tried to find in it the manifestation of a new social conscience. *For Whom the Bell Tolls* also was interpreted in this fashion: Hemingway, it was asserted, had come to see the importance of politics. The writer was at last taking sides in the great struggle against Fascism. More recently *The Old Man and the Sea* has elicited praise as representing something more affirmative still. For myself I have to say that these well-intentioned critical excursions seem to me misguided. A writer's social conscience may emerge in his worst books as well as in his best. Regretfully one has to say that there is no necessary connection. The truth of the matter is that *For Whom the Bell Tolls* scarcely satisfied those who were passionately concerned for the Loyalist cause. Hemingway had portrayed some of his Fascists as human beings and he had made some of his Loyalists cruel and vicious. The very strength of the novel, of course, lies in the fact that Hemingway gives us real people in their complexity and in their exasperating mixture of good and evil. But one must go further still in discounting the importance of the politics of the novel. Though Jordan believes in the Loyalist cause and though he is ultimately willing to die for it, still it is plain that what sustains him at the end is what sustains every other Hemingway hero: an insistence on his freedom, an insistence that though he is defeated he shall be defeated on his own terms.

The virtues that Hemingway celebrates are narrower than those celebrated by political liberalism. They are much narrower than those affirmed by Christianity. There should be no illusion about this. But the virtues Hemingway celebrates are ultimately necessary to Christianity, and, as we have seen, they look toward Christianity. For they have everything to do with man's dignity as a free spirit—they are "spiritual" even though the irony is that the creature who yearns after them is in Hemingway's view a dying animal in a purely mechanistic universe.

It is almost as if Hemingway, driven back out of theism, dispossessed of his heritage, insists upon stubbornly defending whatever he has felt could still be held. It is a kind of rear-guard action that he fights. The point comes out clearly enough in his very first novel, *The Sun Also Rises.* As the book ends, Brett is talking to her friend Jake. Jake and Brett should be married to each other. They understand each other. There is a real bond between them. But fate has played one of its ugly tricks. Jake has been emasculated by a wound received in the war. No marriage between them is possible. Yet Brett relies upon Jake, and now, as the novel ends, she has wired him to come to Madrid to be with her. She has just left the young Spanish bullfighter to whom she has been tremendously attracted and whom she has proceeded to seduce. She has, however, almost immediately given him up because she has realized that she will ruin him and because she has told herself that "I'm not going to be one of these bitches that ruins children."

Brett confides to Jake something of the feelings that possess her at having made this gesture of denial. She tells Jake: "You know it makes one feel rather good deciding not to be a bitch," and when Jake says, "Yes," she goes on to say, "It's sort of what we have instead of God." Jake observes dryly that "Some people have God. Quite a lot." But neither he nor Brett has God, nor do most of the characters with whom Hemingway concerns himself. And perhaps this very honesty, this lack of sentimentality, this refusal to mix up categories, is the thing which makes Hemingway most useful to the reader who does have a religious commitment. Even men and women who do not have God must try to make up for him in some sense, quixotic as that gesture will seem and, in ultimate terms at least, desperate as that gesture must be. The Christian will feel that it is ultimately desperate in that man can never find anything that will prove a substitute for God. But the Christian will do well to recognize his God though hidden by the incognito which He sometimes assumes. Jake's courage is such an incognito and manifests the divine reality, though of course not fully and not in specifically religious terms.

Hemingway is perfectly right to confine himself to his secular terms. Artistic integrity, fidelity to his vision of reality, honesty in portraying the reactions of the Jakes and Bretts of our world—all conduce to this proper limitation. The Christian reader will therefore be very imperceptive if he fails to see how honestly and sensitively Hemingway has portrayed a situation that exists; he will show an unconscionable smugness if he fails to appreciate the gallantry of actions taken in full consciousness that there is no God to approve or sanction them. He will even hesitate to say "There but for the grace of God go I." For it might be presumptuous of him to assume that, deprived of grace, he could go at all along the road that Hemingway's lonely heroes are forced to take.

3.

WILLIAM FAULKNER

VISION OF GOOD AND EVIL

Professor Randall Stewart, in his very stimulating little book *American Literature and Christian Doctrine*, asserts that "Faulkner embodies and dramatizes the basic Christian concepts so effectively that he can with justice be regarded as one of the most profoundly Christian writers in our time. There is everywhere in his writings the basic premise of Original Sin: everywhere the conflict between the flesh and the spirit. One finds also the necessity of discipline, of trial by fire in the furnace of affliction, of sacrifice and the sacrificial death, of redemption through sacrifice. Man in Faulkner is a heroic, tragic figure." This is a view with which I am in basic sympathy. I agree heartily with Professor Stewart on the matter of Faulkner's concern with what he calls "original sin," and with Faulkner's emphasis upon discipline, sacrifice, and redemption. But to call Faulkner "one of the most profoundly Christian writers in our time" seems somewhat incautious. Perhaps it would be safer to say that Faulkner is a profoundly religious writer; that his characters come out of a Christian environment, and represent, whatever their shortcomings and whatever their theological heresies, Christian concerns; and that they are finally to be understood only by reference to Christian premises.

Probably the best place to start is with the term "original sin." The point of reference might very well be T. E. Hulme, one of the profoundly seminal influences on our time, though a critic and philosopher whom Faulkner probably never read. In "Humanism and the Religious Attitude" Hulme argued for a return to orthodox doctrine. His concern with religion, however, had nothing to do with recapturing what he called "the sentiment of Fra Angelico." Rather, "What is important," he asserted, "is what nobody seems to realize—the dogmas like that of Original Sin, which are the closest expression of the categories of the religious attitude. That man is in no sense perfect, but a wretched creature, who can apprehend perfection. It is not, then, that I put up with the dogma for the sake of the sentiment, but that I may possibly swallow the sentiment for the sake of the dogma."

Hulme's position as stated here would seem to smack of scholastic Calvinism rather than of the tradition of Catholic Christianity. His emphasis at least suggests that nature is radically evil and not merely gone wrong somehow—corrupted by a fall. But if Hulme's passage is so tinged, that very fact may make it the more relevant to Faulkner, who shows, in some aspects, the influence of Southern Puritanism.

Be that as it may, Hulme's is not a didactic theory of literature, which stresses some direct preachment to be made. On the contrary, his "classicism" derives from a clear distinction between religious doctrine and poetic structure. It is romantic poetry which blurs that distinction, competing with religion by trying to drag in the infinite. With romanticism we enter the area of "spilt religion," and romantic "damp and fugginess." For Hulme, the classic attitude involves a recognition of man's limitations—his finitude. Since the classical view of man recognizes his limitations and does not presume upon them, the classical attitude, Hulme argues, is a religious attitude. For Hulme is quite convinced that man, though capable of recognizing goodness, is not naturally good. It is only by discipline that he can achieve something of value.

The whole point is an important one, for Faulkner's positive beliefs are often identified with some kind of romantic primitivism. Thus his concern with idiots and children and uneducated rural people, both white and Negro, is sometimes interpreted to mean that man is made evil only by his environment with its corrupting restrictions and inhibitions, and that if man could only realize his deeper impulses, he would be good.[1]

Allied to this misconception is another, namely that Faulkner's characters have no power of choice, being merely the creatures of their drives and needs, and that they are determined by their environment and are helplessly adrift upon the tides of circumstance. It is true that many of his characters are obsessed creatures or badly warped by traumatic experiences, or that they are presented by Faulkner as acting under some kind of compulsion. But his characters are not mere products of an environment. They have the power of choice, they make decisions, and they win their goodness through effort and discipline.

If Faulkner does not believe that man is naturally good and needs only to realize his natural impulses, and if he does believe that man has free will and must act responsibly and discipline himself, then these beliefs are indeed worth stressing, for they are calculated to separate him sharply from writers of a more naturalistic and secularistic temper. But I grant that to attribute to Faulkner a belief in original sin or in man's need for discipline

[1] Faulkner, a few years ago, in defining his notion of Christianity, called it a "code of behavior by means of which (man) makes himself a better human being than his nature wants to be, if he follows his nature only" (*Paris Review*, Spring 1956, p. 42).

would not necessarily prove him a Christian. The concept of grace, for example, is either lacking or at least not clearly evident in Faulkner's work.

Let us begin, then, by examining Faulkner's criticism of secularism and rationalism. A very important theme in his earlier work is the discovery of evil, which is part of man's initiation into the nature of reality. That brilliant and horrifying early novel *Sanctuary* is, it seems to me, to be understood primarily in terms of such an initiation. Horace Benbow is the sentimental idealist, the man of academic temper, who finds out that the world is not a place of moral tidiness or even of justice. He discovers with increasing horror that evil is rooted in the very nature of things. As an intellectual, he likes to ponder meanings and events, he has a great capacity for belief in ideas, and a great confidence in the efficacy of reason. What he comes to discover is the horrifying presence of evil, its insidiousness, and its penetration of every kind of rational or civilized order. There is in this story, to be sure, the unnatural rape of the seventeen-year-old girl by the gangster Popeye, and the story of Popeye's wanton murder of Tommy, but Horace Benbow might conceivably accept both of these things as the kinds of cruel accidents to which human life is subject. What crumples him up is the moral corruption of the girl, which follows on her rape: she actually accepts her life in the brothel and testifies at the trial in favor of the man who had abducted her. What Horace also discovers is that the forces of law and order are also corruptible. His opponent in the trial, the district attorney, plays fast and loose with the evidence and actually ensures that the innocent man will not only be convicted but burned to death by a mob. And what perhaps Horace himself does not discover (but it is made plainly evident to the reader) is that Horace's betrayal at the trial is finally a bosom betrayal: Horace's own sister gives the district attorney the tip-off that will allow him to defeat her brother and make a mockery of justice. Indeed, Horace's sister, the calm and serene Narcissa, is, next to Popeye, the most terrifying person in the novel. She simply does not want her brother associated with people like the accused man, Lee Goodwin, the bootlegger, and his common-law wife. She exclaims to her brother, "I don't see that it makes any difference who [committed the murder]. The question is, are you going to stay mixed up with it?" And she sees to it with quiet and efficient ruthlessness that the trial ends at the first possible date, even though this costs an innocent man's life.

Sanctuary is clearly Faulkner's bitterest novel. It is a novel in which the initiation which every male must undergo is experienced in its most shattering and disillusioning form. Horace not only discovers the existence of evil: he experiences it, not as an abstract idea but as an integral portion of reality. After he has had his interview with Temple Drake in the brothel, he thinks: "Perhaps it is upon the instant that we realize, admit, that there is a logical pattern to evil, that we die," and he thinks of the expression he had once seen in the eyes of a dead child and in the eyes of the other dead: "the cooling indignation, the shocked despair fading, leaving two empty globes in which the motionless world lurked profoundly in miniature."

One of the most important connections has already been touched upon in what I have said earlier. Horace Benbow's initiation into the nature of reality and the nature of evil is intimately associated with his discovery of the true nature of woman. His discovery is quite typical of Faulkner's male characters. In the Faulknerian notion of things, men have to lose their innocence, confront the hard choice, and through a process of initiation discover reality. The women are already in possession of this knowledge, naturally and instinctively. That is why in moments of bitterness Faulkner's male characters—Mr. Compson in *The Sound and the Fury*, for example—assert that women are not innocent. Mr. Compson tells his son Quentin: "Women are like that[;] they don't acquire knowledge of people[. Men] are for that[. Women] are just born with a practical fertility of suspicion. . . . they have an affinity for evil[—]for supplying whatever the evil lacks in itself[—]drawing it about them instinctively as you do bed clothing in slumber. . . ." Again, "Women only use other people's codes of honour."

I suppose that we need not take these Schopenhauerian profundities of the bourbon-soaked Mr. Compson too seriously. It might on the whole be more accurate to say that Faulkner's women lack the callow idealism of the men, have fewer illusions about human nature, and are less trammeled by legalistic distinctions and niceties of any code of conduct.

Faulkner's view of women, then, is radically old-fashioned—even medieval. Woman is the source and sustainer of virtue and also a prime source of evil. She can be either, because she is, as man is not, always a little beyond good and evil. With her powerful natural drives and her instinct for the concrete and personal, she does not need to agonize over her decisions. There is no code for her to master—no initiation for her to undergo. For this reason she has access to a wisdom which is veiled from man; and man's codes, good or bad, are always, in their formal abstraction, a little absurd in her eyes. Women are close to nature; the feminine principle is closely related to the instinctive and natural: woman typically manifests pathos rather than ethos.

A little later I shall have something more to say about Faulkner's characters in confrontation with nature. At this point, however, I want to go back and refer to another aspect of *Sanctuary*. The worst villains in Faulkner are cut off from nature. They have in some profound way denied their nature, like Flem Snopes in *The Hamlet*, who has no natural vices, only the unnatural vice of a pure lust for power and money. In *Sanctuary* Popeye is depicted as a sort of *ludus naturae*. Everybody has noticed the way in which he is described, as if he were a kind of automaton, with eyes like "two knobs of soft black rubber." As Horace watches him across the spring, Popeye's "face had a queer, bloodless color, as though seen by electric light; against the sunny silence, in his slanted straw hat and his slightly akimbo arms, he had that vicious depthless quality of stamped tin." Faulkner's two figures of speech are brilliantly used here. They serve to rob Popeye of substance and to turn him into a sinister black silhouette against the spring landscape. The phrase "as though seen by electric light" justifies the description of his queer, bloodless color, but it does more than this. Juxtaposed as it is to the phrase "against the sunny silence," it stresses the sense of the contrived, the artificial, as though Popeye constituted a kind of monstrous affront to the natural scene. These suggestions of a shadowy lack of substance are confirmed at the end of the sentence with the closing phrase: "depthless quality of stamped tin." Faulkner relentlessly forces this notion of the unnatural: Popeye deliberately spits into the spring, he cringes in terror from the low swooping owl, he is afraid of the dark.

Popeye has no natural vices either. He cannot drink. Since he is impotent, he is forced to use unnatural means in his rape of Temple. As a consequence, some readers take Popeye to be a kind of allegorical figure, a representation of the inhumanly mechanistic forces of our society. We may say that Popeye is quite literally a monster, remembering that the Latin *monstrum* signifies something that lies outside the ordinary course of nature.

Though Popeye represents an extreme case, in this matter he is typical of all of Faulkner's villains. For example, Thomas Sutpen, in *Absalom, Absalom!*, is a man of great courage and heroic stature, who challenges the role of a tragic protagonist. Yet he has about him this same rigid and mechanical quality. Sutpen, as an acquaintance observes, believes "that the ingredients of morality were like the ingredients of pie or cake and once you had measured them and balanced them and mixed them and put them into the oven it was all finished and nothing but pie or cake could come out."

Sutpen has a great plan in mind, his "design," he calls it—which involves his building a great plantation house and setting up a dynasty. As he tells General Compson, "I had a design. To accomplish it I should require money, a house, and a plantation, slaves, a family—incidentally, of course, a wife." But when he finds later that his wife has a trace of Negro blood, he puts her aside, and he does it with an air of honest grievance. He says "[Her parents] deliberately withheld from me the one fact which I have reason to know they were aware would have caused me to decline the entire matter, otherwise they would not have withheld it from me—a fact which I did not learn until after my son was born. And even then I did not act hastily. I could have reminded them of these wasted years, these years which would now leave me behind with my schedule. . . ." (The last term is significant: Sutpen, modern man that he is, works in accordance with a timetable.) He tells General Compson that when he put aside his wife and child, "his conscience had bothered him somewhat at first but that he had argued calmly and logically with his conscience until it was settled." General Compson is aghast at this revelation of moral myopia. He calls it "innocence," and by the term he means a blindness to the nature of reality. And since the writer is Faulkner, the blindness involves a blindness to the nature of woman. For Sutpen has actually believed that by providing a more than just property settlement he could reconcile his wife to his abandoning her. General Compson had thrown up his hands and exclaimed: "Good God, man . . . what kind of conscience [did you have] to trade with which would have warranted you in the belief that you could have bought immunity from her for no other coin but justice?—"

Evil for Faulkner, then, involves a violation of nature and runs counter to the natural appetites and affections. And yet, as we have seen, the converse is not true; Faulkner does not consider the natural and instinctive and impulsive as automatically and necessarily good. Here I think rests the best warrant for maintaining that Faulkner holds an orthodox view of man and reality. For his men, at least, cannot be content merely with being natural. They cannot live merely by their instincts and natural appetites. They must confront the fact of evil. They are constrained to moral choices. They have to undergo a test of their courage, in making and abiding by the choice. They achieve goodness by discipline and effort. This proposition is perhaps most fully and brilliantly illustrated in Faulkner's story "The Bear." Isaac McCaslin, when he comes of age, decides to repudiate his inheritance. He refuses to accept his father's plantation and chooses to earn his living as a carpenter and to live in a rented room. There are two powerful motives that shape this decision: the sacramental view of nature which he has been taught by the old hunter, Sam Fathers, and the discovery of his grandfather's guilt in his treatment of one of his slaves: the grandfather had incestuously begotten a child upon his own half-Negro daughter.

"The Bear" is thus a story of penance and expiation, as also of a difficult moral decision made and maintained, but since it is so well known and has received so much commentary, I want to illustrate Faulkner's characteristic drama of moral choice from a less familiar story, "An Odor of Verbena," which is the concluding section of Faulkner's too little appreciated but brilliant novel *The Unvanquished.* As this episode opens, word has come to Bayard Sartoris, a young man of twenty-four off at law school, that his father has been assassinated by a political enemy. Ringo, the young Negro man of his own age and his boyhood companion, has ridden to the little town where Bayard is at law school to bring the news. Bayard knows what is expected of him—the date is 1874, the tradition of the code of honor still lingers. the devastating Civil War and the Reconstruction have contorted the land with violence, and Bayard knows that the community expects him to call his father's assassin to account. Even the quiet and gentle Judge Wilkins with whom he is studying law expects him to do so, and though he speaks to the boy with pity ("Bayard, my son, my dear son"), he offers him not only his horse but his pistol as well. Certainly also Bayard's father's Civil War troop expect him to avenge his father. Bayard's young stepmother, eight years older than he, expects it. Speaking in a "silvery ecstatic voice" like the priestess of a rite wrought up to a point of hysteria, she offers Bayard the pistols when he returns to the family home. Even Ringo expects it.

Some years before, when Bayard and Ringo were sixteen, at the very end of the Civil War, when the region had become a no-man's land terrorized by bushwhackers, Bayard's grandmother had been killed by a ruffian named Grumby, and Bayard and Ringo had followed him for weeks until finally they had run him down and killed him. Bayard had loved his grandmother, and was resolved that her murderer should be punished. But there was no law and order in this troubled time to which he could appeal; the two sixteen-year-old boys had to undertake the punishment themselves.

Now as the two young men ride back to Jefferson, Ringo says to Bayard, "We could bushwhack him.... Like we done Grumby that day. But I reckon that wouldn't suit that white skin you walks around in." Bayard in fact has resolved that he will not kill again.

The motive for this decision is complex. For one thing, he realizes that his father had become a proud and abstracted and ruthless man. Bayard had loved his father but is well aware that his father had pressed his opponent, Redmond, far too hard. George Wyatt, the countryman who had served under his father, earlier had in fact come to Bayard to ask him to restrain his father: "'Right or wrong,' he said, 'us boys and most of the other folks in this county know John's right. But he ought to let Redmond alone. I know what's wrong: he's had to kill too many folks, and that's bad for a man. We all know Colonel's brave as a lion, but Redmond ain't no coward either and they ain't any use in making a brave man that made one mistake eat crow all the time. Can't you talk to him?'"

Another powerful motive is evidently the psychic wound that Bayard has suffered in the killing of Grumby. He has executed vengeance once, and in that instance there were extenuating circumstances to justify his taking the law into his own hands. But this case is different, and as he says to himself before he begins his journey home, "If there [is] anything at all in the Book, anything of hope and peace for [God's] blind and bewildered spawn," the command "'*Thou Shalt not kill*' must be it." Finally, and not least, there is the example of his own father. Even his father had decided that there had been too much killing. Two months before, he had told Bayard: "Now I shall do a little moral house cleaning. I am tired of killing men, no matter what the necessity or the end." Thus Bayard, in resolving not to avenge his father, may be said to be following his father's own resolve.

But Bayard, as a member of a tightly knit community, does not want to be branded as a coward; he respects his community's opinion, and he feels compelled to live up to what the community expects of him. And so he resolves, though the reader does not learn of it until late in the story, to face Redmond, but to face him unarmed.

There is one person who understands his dilemma and can support him in his decision. It is his Aunt Jenny, who tells him when he arrives home that night: "'Yes. All right. Don't let it be Drusilla, poor hysterical young woman. And don't let it be [your father], Bayard, because he's dead now. And don't let it be George Wyatt and those others who will be waiting for you tomorrow morning. I know you are not afraid.' 'But what good will that do?' I said. 'What good will that do?' . . . 'I must live with myself, you see.' 'Then it's not just Drusilla? Not just him? Not just George Wyatt and Jefferson?' 'No,' I said."

It is indeed not just Drusilla and George Wyatt and the other outsiders that are forcing Bayard to take his proposed course of action. As he tells his aunt, it is not enough that *she* knows that he is not afraid. He must prove it to himself. "I must live with myself," he says. This is the situation of many a Faulkner character. He must live with himself. He must prove to himself that he possesses the requisite courage.

Bayard is fortunate. The man that he goes to meet is also brave, also decent. He has decided that, having killed the father, he will not kill the young son. Thus, when Bayard walks up the stairs past the small faded sign "*B. J. Redmond. Atty at Law*" and opens the door, he sees Redmond sitting "behind the desk, not much taller than Father, but thicker as a man gets that spends most of his time sitting and listening to people, freshly shaven and with fresh linen; a lawyer yet it was not a lawyer's face—a face much thinner than the body would indicate, strained (and yes, tragic; I know that now) and exhausted beneath the neat recent steady strokes of the razor, holding a pistol flat on the desk before him, loose beneath his hand and aimed at nothing." Redmond fires twice but Bayard can see that the gun was not aimed at him and that the misses are deliberate. Then Redmond gets up from his desk, blunders down the stairs and walks on out past George Wyatt and the six other members of Colonel Sartoris' old troop. He "walked through the middle of them with his hat on and his head up (they told me how someone shouted at him: 'Have you killed that boy too?' saying no word, staring straight ahead and with his back to them, on to the station where the south-bound train was just in and got on it with no baggage, nothing, and went away from Jefferson and from Mississippi and never came back."

George Wyatt rushes up to Bayard, mistakenly thinking that he had taken Redmond's pistol away from him and then missed him, missed him twice. "Then he answered himself . . . 'No; wait. You walked in here without even a pocket knife and let him miss you twice. My God in heaven.'" But he adds, "'You ain't done anything to be ashamed of. I wouldn't have done it that way, myself. I'd a shot at him once, anyway. But that's your way or you wouldn't have done it." And even Drusilla, the wrought-up priestess of violence, before she leaves the house forever to go back to her kinsfolk in Alabama, leaves on Bayard's pillow a sprig of verbena because it is the odor of courage, "that odor which she said you could smell alone above the smell of horses," as a token that she too has accepted his act as brave and honorable.

One further observation: as I have already remarked, it is the men who have to be initiated into the meaning of reality, who have to observe a code of conduct, who have to prove themselves worthy. Aunt Jenny, as a woman, is outside the code. Indeed she sees the code as absurd and quixotic, though she knows that Bayard as a man will have to observe it. And what shall we say of Drusilla, who is a woman, and yet is the very high priestess of the code? Drusilla is the masculinized woman, who as a type occurs more than once in Faulkner. Drusilla's story is that she has lost her fiancé early in the war and finally in her boredom and despair has actually ridden with the Confederate cavalry. She is brave and Faulkner gives her her due, but he is not celebrating her as a kind of Confederate Joan of Arc. Her action exacts its penalty and she ends a warped and twisted woman, truly a victim of the war.

I realize that I am risking oversimplification in pressing some of these issues so hard—for example, the contrast between man and woman, in their relation to nature and to their characteristic roles as active and passive. One may be disposed to doubt that even a traditional writer writing about a traditional society would stylize these relationships as much as I have suggested Faulkner has. Yet I am very anxious to sketch in, even at the risk of over-bold strokes, the general nature of Faulkner's conception of good and evil, and so I mean to stand by this summary: Faulkner sees the role of man as active; man makes choices and lives up to the choices. Faulkner sees the role of woman as characteristically fostering and sustaining. She undergirds society, upholding the family and community mores, sending her men out into battle, including the ethical battle. This generalization I believe, is, if oversimplified, basically true. And I should like to relate it to Faulkner's "Calvinistic" Protestantism. In so far as his Calvinism represents a violent repression and constriction of natural impulse, a denial of nature itself, Faulkner tends to regard it as a terrible and evil thing. And the natural foil to characters who have so hardened their hearts in accordance with their notion of a harsh and vindictive God is the feminine principle as exemplified by a person like Lena Grove, the heroine of *Light in August*. Lena has a childlike confidence in herself and in mankind. She is a creature of warm natural sympathies and a deep instinctive commitment to her natural function.

But Faulkner has still another relation to Calvinistic Protestantism. Insofar as the tradition insists that man must be brought up to the urgency of decision, must be set tests of courage and endurance, must have his sinews strung tight for some moral leap or his back braced so as to stand firm against the push of circumstance, Faulkner evidently derives from this tradition. From it may be derived the very necessity that compels his male characters to undergo an initiation. The required initiation may be analogous to the crisis of conversion and the character's successful entrance into knowledge of himself, analogous to the sinner's experiencing salvation.

On the conscious level, Faulkner is obviously a Protestant

anticleric, fascinated, but also infuriated, by some of the more violently repressive features of the religion that dominates his country. This matter is easily illustrated. One of his masterpieces, *Light in August*, provides a stinging criticism of the harsher aspects of Protestantism. Indeed a basic theme in *Light in August* is man's strained attempt to hold himself up in a rigid aloofness above the relaxed female world. The struggle to do so is, as Faulkner portrays it in this novel, at once monstrous, comic, and heroic, as the various characters take up their special postures.

In a character like old Doc Hines, there is a definite distortion and perversion. His fury at "bitchery and abomination" is the fury of a crazed man. In her conversation with Bunch and Hightower, Mrs. Hines states quite precisely what has happened to her husband: he began "then to take God's name in vain and in pride to justify and excuse the devil that was in him." His attribution of his furies to God is quite literally a taking of God's name in vain, blasphemy. The tendency to call one's own hates the vengeance of a just God is a sin to which Protestantism has always been prone. But not merely Southern Protestantism and, of course, not merely Protestantism as such.

Calvin Burden represents another instance of the militant Protestant, but this man's heartiness and boisterous energy have something of the quality of comedy. He is the son of a Unitarian minister; but when he runs away to the West, he becomes a Roman Catholic and lives for a year in a monastery. Then, on his marriage, he repudiates the Catholic Church, choosing for the scene of his formal repudiation "a saloon, insisting that every one present listen to him and state their objections." Then, though he cannot read the English Bible—he had learned from the priests in California to read Spanish—he begins to instruct his child in the true religion, interspersing his readings to the child in Spanish with "extemporised dissertations composed half of the bleak and bloodless logic which he remembered from his father on interminable New England Sundays and half of immediate hellfire and tangible brimstone." Perhaps he differs from the bulk of doctrinaire hellfire and brimstone Protestants in not being a "proselyter" or a "missionary." But everything else marks him as truly of the breed: his intensity, his stern authoritarianism, and his violence. He has killed a man in an argument over slavery and he threatens to "frail the tar" out of his children if they do not learn to hate what he hates—hell and slaveholders.

The case of the Rev. Gail Hightower is one of the most interesting of all. He is the only one of these Protestants who has had formal theological training. Because of that fact one might expect him to be the most doctrinaire. He is not. He seems at the beginning of the book the most tolerant and pitying of all the characters, the one who recoils in horror at man's capacity for evil and man's propensity to crucify his fellows: he is a man whose only defense against violence is nonresistance. One may be inclined to say that Hightower had rebelled against his Calvinist training and repudiated the jealous and repressive God. Certainly, there is truth in this notion. Hightower is a disillusioned man and a man who has learned something from his sufferings. But there is a sense in which he has never broken out of the mold: he still stresses a God of justice rather than of mercy, for his sincerest belief is that he has somehow "bought immunity." He exclaims: "I have paid. I have paid"—in confidence that God is an honest merchant who has receipted his bill and will honor his title to the precious merchandise he has purchased at such cost.

Lastly there is the case of Joe Christmas, the violent rebel against hellfire Protestantism. His detachment from any kind of human community is shocking. Here is a man who has no family ties, no continuity with the past, no place in any community whatsoever. He is a man who has literally tried to kick the earth out from under his feet. Yet his very alienation and his insistence upon his own individual integrity are touched with the tragically heroic. As a child he is conscious that he is being hounded by old Doc Hines; he resists stubbornly the discipline imposed by his foster father McEachern, whom he finally brains with a chair; and when his paramour, Joanna Burden, threatens him with hell and insists that he kneel with her and pray for forgiveness, he decapitates her. Yet there is a most important sense in which Joe Christmas is the sternest and most doctrinaire Calvinist in the book.

He imbibes more from the training of his foster father than he realizes. For all that he strains in fierce resistance against him, he "could depend" on "the hard, just, ruthless man." It is the "soft kindness" of the woman, his foster mother that he abominates. If one mark of the Calvinists in this novel is their fear and distrust of women and their hatred of the female principle, then Joe Christmas is eminently qualified to take a place among them. He even has affinities with his old childhood ogre, Doc Hines, and Hines' fury at the bitchery of women and the abomination of Negro blood. Joe, hearing the "fecundmellow" voices of Negro women, feels that he and "all other manshaped life about him" had been returned to the "lightless hot wet primogenitive Female" and runs from the scene in a kind of panic.

Christmas too wants not mercy but justice, is afraid of the claims of love and its obligations, and yearns only for a vindication of his identity and integrity—a vindication made the more difficult by his not really knowing precisely what he would vindicate. When he puts aside the temptation to marry Joanna and win ease and security, he does it by saying: "If I give in now, I will deny all the thirty years that I have lived to make me what I chose to be." Finally, Joe is something of a fatalist, and his fatalism is a kind of perversion of Calvinist determinism. On his way to murder Joanna, "he believed with calm paradox that he was the volitionless servant of the fatality in which he believed that he did not believe." But so "fated" is his act of murder that he keeps saying to himself "I had to do it"—using the past tense, as if the act had already been performed.

Lena (along with Eula of *The Hamlet*) has sometimes been called an earth goddess. The description does have a certain aptness when applied to Eula, especially in some of the more rhapsodic passages of *The Hamlet*. But it is a little highfalutin for Lena. It is more accurate to say that Lena is one of Faulkner's several embodiments of the female principle—indeed one of the purest and least complicated of his embodiments. Her rapport with nature is close. She is never baffled as to what course of action to take. She is never torn by doubts and indecisions. There is no painful introspection. This serene composure has frequently been put down to sheer mindlessness, and Lena, to be sure, is a very simple young woman. But Faulkner himself undoubtedly attributes most of Lena's quiet force to her female nature. In this novel the principal male characters suffer alienation. They are separated from the community, are in rebellion against it—and against nature. But Lena moves serenely into the community, and it gathers itself about her with protective gestures. Its response to her, of course, is rooted in a deep and sound instinct: Lena embodies the principle upon which any human community is founded. She is the carrier of life and she has to be protected and nurtured if there is to be any human community at all.

I have said that *Light in August* depicts man's strained attempt to hold himself up in rigid aloofness above the relaxed female world. In terms of the plot, Lena is the direct means by which Byron Bunch and the indirect means by which Hightower are redeemed from their pallid half lives and brought back into the community. This coming back into the community is an essential part of the redemption. Unless the controlling purposes of the individuals are related to those that other men share, and in which the individual can participate, he is indeed isolated, and is forced to fall back upon his personal values, with all the risk of fanaticism and distortion to which such isolation is liable.

The community is at once the field for man's action and the norm by which his action is judged and regulated. It sometimes seems that the sense of an organic community has all but disappeared from modern fiction, and the disappearance accounts for the terrifying self-consciousness and subjectivity of a great deal of modern writing. That Faulkner has some sense of an organic community still behind him is among his most important resources as a writer.

In *Light in August* Faulkner uses Lena to confirm an ideal of integrity and wholeness in the light of which the alienated characters are judged; and this is essentially the function of Dilsey, the Negro servant in *The Sound and the Fury*, regarded by many people as Faulkner's masterpiece. Dilsey's role, to be sure, is more positive than Lena's. She has affinities not with the pagan goddess but with the Christian saint. She is not the young woman and young mother that Lena is. She is an older woman and an older mother, and she is the sustaining force—the only possible sustaining force of a broken and corrupted family.

Yet Dilsey's primary role is generally similar to Lena's: she affirms the ideal of wholeness in a family which shows in every other member splintering and disintegration. *The Sound and the Fury* can be regarded as a study in the fragmentation of modern man. There is Benjy, the idiot brother who represents the life of the instincts and the unreflective emotions; there is Quentin, the intellectual and artistic brother, who is conscious of his own weakness and failure and yet so hagridden by impossible ideals that he finally turns away from life altogether and commits suicide; and there is Jason, the brother who represents an aggressive and destructive rationalism that dissolves all family and community loyalties and attachments. There has been a somewhat strained attempt to portray the brothers in Freudian terms:

Benjy as the *id*, Quentin as the tortured *ego*, and Jason as the tyrannical and cruel *super-ego*. Faulkner's own way of regarding the three brothers (as implied in the appendix he supplied for the Modern Library edition) is interesting. Benjy is an idiot, of course; Quentin, in his obsession, is obviously half-mad; and Jason is perfectly sane, the first "sane" Compson for generations. Faulkner's mocking choice of the term "sane" to characterize Jason's coldly monstrous self-serving (all of Faulkner's villains, let me repeat, are characterized by this devouring and destructive rationalism) is highly significant. It is as if Faulkner argued that mere sanity were not enough—indeed that pure sanity was inhuman. The good man has to transcend his mere intellect with some overflow of generosity and love.

But we ought not to confine ourselves to the three brothers, for Dilsey is being contrasted not merely with them but with the whole of the family. There is Mr. Compson, who has been defeated by life and has sunk into whisky and fatalism. There is Mrs. Compson, the mother, whom Faulkner calls a "cold, weak" person. She is the whining, self-centred hypochondriac who has poisoned the whole family relationship. She is evidently a primary cause of her husband's cynicism; she has spoiled and corrupted her favorite son, Jason; and she has withheld her love from the other children. Quentin, on the day of his suicide, can say to himself bitterly, "If I only had a mother." Mrs. Compson is all that Dilsey is not. It is the mother role that she has abandoned that Dilsey is compelled to assume. There is lastly the daughter of the family, Candace, who in her own way also represents the dissolution of the family. Candace has become a wanton. Sex is her particular escape from an unsatisfactory home, and she is subject to her own kind of specialization, the semiprofessionalism of a sexual adventuress.

In contrast with this splintered family, Dilsey maintains a wholeness. Indeed, Dilsey's wholeness constitutes her holiness.

(It is well to remember that *whole* and *holy* are related and come from the same root.) In Dilsey the life of the instincts, including the sex drive, the life of the emotions, and the life of ideal values and of rationality are related meaningfully to one another. To say this is to say, of course, that Dilsey is a profoundly religious person. Her life with its round of daily tasks and responsibilities is related to the larger life of eternity and eternal values. Dilsey does not have to strain to make meaningful some particular desire or dream or need. Her world is a solid and meaningful world. It is filled with pain, toil, and difficulty, but it is not wrenched by agonizing doubts and perplexities.

I said a moment ago that Dilsey was sometimes compared to the saint and in what I am going to say I do not mean to deprive her of her properly deserved halo. But we must not allow the term to sentimentalize her. If she treats with compassion the idiot Benjy, saying "You's de Lawd's chile, anyway," she is quite capable of dealing summarily with her own child, Luster, when he needs a rebuke: "Lemme tell you somethin, nigger boy, you got jes es much Compson devilment in you es any of em. Is you right sho you never broke dat window?" Dilsey's earthiness and her human exasperations are very much in evidence in this novel. Because they are, Dilsey's "saintliness" is altogether credible and convincing.

One may say in general of Faulkner's Negroes that they remain close to a concrete world of values—less perverted by abstraction—more honest in recognizing what is essential and elemental than are most of the white people. Faulkner certainly does not assume any inherent virtue in the Negro race. But he does find among his Negro characters less false pride, less false idealism, more seasoned discipline in the elemental human relationships. The Negro virtues which Faulkner praises in "The Bear" are endurance, patience, honesty, courage, and the love of children—white or black. Dilsey, then, is not a primitive figure who through some mystique of race or healthiness of natural impulses is good. Dilsey is unsophisticated and warm-hearted, but she is no noble savage. Her role is in its general dimensions comparable to that of her white sisters such as the matriarchs Aunt Jenny and Mrs. Rosa Millard, fostering and sustaining forces. If she goes beyond them in exemplifying the feminine principle at its best, still hers is no mere goodness by and of nature, if one means by this a goodness that justifies a faith in man as man. Dilsey does not believe in man; she believes in God.

To try for a summary of a very difficult and complicated topic: Evil for Faulkner involves the violation of the natural and the denial of the human. As Isaac's older kinsman says in "The Bear," "Courage and honor and pride, and pity and love of justice and of liberty. They all touch the heart, and what the heart holds to becomes truth, as far as we know truth." A meanness of spirit and coldness of calculation which would deny the virtues that touch the heart is by that very fact proven false. Yet Faulkner is no disciple of Jean-Jacques Rousseau. He has no illusions that man is naturally good or that he can safely trust to his instincts and emotions. Man is capable of evil, and this means that goodness has to be achieved by struggle and discipline and effort. Like T. S. Eliot, Faulkner has small faith in social arrangements so perfectly organized that nobody has to take the trouble to be good. Finally Faulkner's noblest characters are willing to face the fact that most men can learn the deepest truths about themselves and about reality only through suffering. Hurt and pain and loss are not mere accidents to which the human being is subject; nor are they mere punishments incurred by human error; they can be the means to the deeper knowledge and to the more abundant life.

4.
W. B. YEATS
SEARCH FOR A NEW MYTH

William Butler Yeats is recognized today as one of the great poets of the last two centuries. Yet in spite of the fact that he has an international reputation, he bears a very special relation to a particular provincial culture. Compare him for a moment with another modern writer, William Faulkner. Yeats and Faulkner perhaps strike one as thoroughly dissimilar figures, and yet the situations in which they found themselves are oddly alike. Both writers display a concern for regionalism; both are tremendously concerned with the past; and both have criticized the prevailing commercial and urban culture from the standpoint of a provincial and minority culture.

Like Faulkner, Yeats benefited immeasurably from the fact that his own country, Ireland, showed a long cultural lag behind the great commercial and intellectual centers like London and New York. Again, as with Faulkner, it is easy to make the superficial accusation that Yeats' work, particularly his early work, is romantic, escapist, defeatist, and in retreat from the modern world. But surely his mature work is as tough as whipcord, and his protest against the modern tendencies that destroy man's personality and emasculate his soul are realistic and pointed and knowing. As with Faulkner, Yeats' sense of history and his sense of a tradition are important, and with Yeats one can go further to say that the traditionalism is based upon a wide reading in, and a rich knowledge of, Plato and Plotinus, Berkeley and Vico, and the modern cultural historians. Yeats' judgment of our age sums itself up in his indictment of what he calls "Whiggery," and I cannot do better than to quote his own definition of it from his poem called "The Seven Sages." These sages are old men talking about Ireland and her history. In the lines I shall quote, the fifth, the sixth, and the seventh sages speak.

> *The Fifth.* Whence came our thought?
> *The Sixth.* From four great minds that hated Whiggery.
> *The Fifth.* Burke was a Whig.
> *The Sixth.* Whether they knew or not,
> Goldsmith and Burke, Swift and the Bishop
> of Cloyne
> All hated Whiggery; but what is Whiggery?
> A levelling, rancorous, rational sort of mind
> That never looked out of the eye of a saint
> Or out of a drunkard's eye.
> *The Seventh.* All's Whiggery now,
> But we old men are massed against the world.

Or again, Yeats suggests the nature of the curse that hovers over the modern world in these lines from "Meditations: In Time of Civil War":

> . . . eyes that rage has brightened, arms it has made lean,
> Give place to an indifferent multitude, give place
> To brazen hawks. Nor self-delighting reverie,
> Nor hate of what's to come, nor pity for what's gone,
> Nothing but grip of claw, and the eye's complacency,
> The innumerable clanging wings that have put out the moon.

Yeats is more directly philosophical than Hemingway or Faulkner. He is more obviously intellectual than either of them. Moreover, he represents an intellectual situation typical of a generation earlier, for Yeats did not so much inherit a Christianity under attack or actually repudiated and abandoned, as we might say of Hemingway and Faulkner. On the contrary, Yeats felt that he was robbed of his religion. At least he could say so later on, when he was writing his *Autobiographies*. He tells us that after a brief enthusiasm for natural science as a boy, he soon came to hate science "with a monkish hate." "I am," he writes in his *Autobiographies*, "very religious, and deprived by Huxley and Tyndall . . . of the simple-minded religion of my childhood, I had made a new religion, almost an infallible church of poetic tradition, of a fardel of stories, and of personages, and of emotions, inseparable from their first expression, passed on from generation to generation by poets and painters with some help from philosophers and theologians."

Yeats from an early period made many attempts to construct this kind of personal religion. The constructions take various forms. The most elaborate and of course most celebrated is that strange mythological system which he published in 1925 in a volume entitled *A Vision*. Not since the prophetic books of William Blake has any poet in English gone so far in elaborating what must be called a private mythology.

In his introduction to *A Vision* Yeats tells us: "I wished for a system of thought that would leave my imagination free to create as it chose and yet make all it created, or could create, part of the one history, and that the soul's." The picture of man and of history which science sanctioned—at least as it seemed to Yeats—was dry, mechanical, impoverished. Yeats yearned for a richer, more imaginative account of man, one from which the poetry had not been squeezed out, one which provided some continuity with the values and symbols of ancient wisdom. But he craved something more coherent than a merely entertaining fairy tale, something more objectively responsible to historical facts than a merely subjective reverie. Yet for Yeats his own inherited religion, Christianity, could not provide it—perhaps because it had been denatured by Victorian compromises, perhaps because it had been directly challenged by Darwin and Huxley—or because it had simply been left "defenseless by a theology which had drowned in rivers of vulgar evangelical piety, or which had blown away on the high ecclesiastical winds of Tractarian romance."[1]

As for *A Vision*, I can but suggest something of the content of that rich, confused, and baffling book. It comprises a history, a psychology, and an account of the purification of the soul after death and the manner by which it is prepared for rebirth in another human body. In the matter of history, *A Vision* most resembles Oswald Spengler's cyclic view of history, though Yeats claimed that he read Spengler only after his own work was substantially finished. Yeats sees history running through two-thousand-year cycles, each cycle reversing the basic trend of the preceding cycle. Yeats finds our own civilization almost at the end of its cycle, and the present time already filled with hints and portents of the new annunciation which will begin the cycle to come.

The psychology employed in *A Vision* is at points curiously like that of Carl Jung, though the parallels are presumably accidental. I certainly cannot argue for any conscious derivation. To give instances: Yeats has four terms in his psychology, even as Jung has, and Yeats believes in a world memory which anticipates rather strikingly Jung's collective unconscious. The poet, for example, draws his great compelling images—Jung would call them archetypes—from this collective world memory, or, as Yeats calls it, the *anima mundi*.

[1] Mr. Charles C. Gillispie is not referring to Yeats specifically here, but is giving an account of the general state of affairs: *Victorian Studies*, *2* (1958), 168.

Yeats' account of the fortunes of the soul after death owes much to Platonism and to Indian philosophy. Here, of course, are to be found the most fantastic aspects of Yeats' system. The system as a whole, he tells us, was dictated by the spirits through his wife's mediumship. And that account itself will be sufficient to disqualify it for most hard-bitten moderns. But extravagant as the book is, Yeats never really loses his hold on reality. And he does not lose his sense of humor. He says two things that make it easier for us to maintain our faith in him: in the first place, according to Yeats, the teaching spirits told him their object was not to instruct him in philosophy but to furnish him metaphors for his poetry. In the second place, Yeats closes his book with the declaration: "I would restore to the philosopher his mythology," and the term he chooses, "mythology," is significant. But Yeats goes on to raise the question of his own belief in his system. To that question he replies with a counterquestion: whether the word "belief," as the questioner will use it, properly belongs to our age. It is a fair question and a discerning question. To sum up, Yeats' fantastic system is frankly a fiction, a myth, but unless we are dogmatic positivists we shall at our peril utterly deny that it purveys truth.

Yeats claims at times that his reconstituted religion is not anti-Christian but includes Christianity. His is the true ancient religion of which Christianity is one branch. This view, of course, is not calculated to satisfy any serious Christian, and it suggests that Yeats misunderstood the true nature of the Christian claim, too easily merging Christianity into the ancient nature religions. Yet it ought to be observed that Yeats at other times seems to commit himself powerfully, if extravagantly, to the extreme Christian claim. In 1924, for example, he advised a group of young Dublin poets to found themselves "on the doctrine of the immortality of the soul, most bishops and all bad writers being obviously atheists."

All bad writers and too many bishops, if I may dare to paraphrase Yeats, oversimplify the human predicament. They deny the mystery always to be found in the human being. They miss the drama of the human soul. This Yeats never does, and if to avoid doing so is to avoid atheism, then Yeats admirably succeeded in avoiding it to the end of his life. I remind you of Tillich's description of the characteristic stance of the artist in our day as one of reaction against those forces in modern culture that would turn man into a mere thing. The description applies in full measure to Yeats. He is constantly affirming that man is not a "thing," that one cannot understand man through any mere mechanical scheme—that understanding him begins with some sense of reverence for his passionate mystery.

A little while ago I referred to Yeats' hatred of Whiggery. His indictment of this "levelling, rancorous, rational sort of mind" involves several particulars. There is, for example, his bitter and pithy comment upon John Locke, English empiricism, and the Industrial Revolution.

> Locke sank into a swoon;
> The Garden died;
> God took the spinning-jenny
> Out of his side.

In this revised genesis the all-too-stuffy founder of British empiricism is the Adam, the Eve is the first mass-production machine, and with its creation ensues the death of the happy garden. Or again, in a scoffing and bitter little occasional poem, Yeats ticks off several pet hates, including journalism and politics.

> A statesman is an easy man,
> He tells his lies by rote;
> A journalist makes up his lies

And takes you by the throat;
So stay at home and drink your beer
And let the neighbours vote. . . .

In spite of the calculated subversiveness of this little squib, to be justified, if at all, I suppose, as the licensed petulance of a crusty old man, Yeats' indictment of modern civilization emerges as a terribly sincere and important one. Systematic vulgarization of man's spiritual life, the insistence that man is a mere animal, the decay of language, a lying and shoddy politics—these are all attacks upon man's spiritual integrity, and upon them Yeats waged unrelenting war throughout a lifetime. The attack upon the corruption of language and the corruption of the spirit is important. Yeats considered it so, and in the last year of his life he wrote:

Nor can there be work so great
As that which cleans man's dirty slate.

But one must grant that such passages as I have been citing do not give a specifically Christian judgment upon modern civilization. They constitute, rather, protests against the general subversion of the humanity of man, a subversion which has gone along with the scientific neutralization of nature.

But there are positive Christian elements in Yeats—in spite of his tendency to see Christianity as simply one branch of a larger traditional religion and in spite of the fact that his later poems tend to see life through the drunkard's eye rather than through the eye of the saint. For the great Christian symbols run throughout his later work; the great Christian doctrines become the reference points for his generalizations or the grounding for his basic metaphors; the great Christian themes often become his very subject matter. And if Yeats is constantly warping them, twisting them, commenting sardonically upon them, or using them as metaphors for profane love, still his very obsession with them tells its own story. These Christian concepts are the very matrix of his thought about the human predicament. Moreover, in saying that Yeats "warps" or "twists" or "comments sardonically" upon the Christian elements, I have been somewhat unfair to my argument and perhaps been unfair to Yeats, for it would be quite as appropriate to say of many of his poems that Yeats is exploring, probing, and reassessing the Christian elements rather than merely rejecting them. Indeed, in his later work there is rarely a simple rejection of any thesis; there is rather a kind of poetic dialectic in which the antithesis is played hard over against the thesis in order to develop a dramatic comment in which the opposites shall both remain alive and valid in a higher synthesis. Thus when the old poet utters a prayer, a prayer which seems to deny the mind and to celebrate the flesh, the prayer is to God, and the poet has gone out of his way to note that he is *praying*.

> I pray—for fashion's word is out
> And prayer comes round again—
> That I may seem, though I die old,
> A foolish, passionate man.

But I can probably make this difficult point most simply by quoting one of Yeats' last poems. The title certainly seems uncompromisingly anti-Christian, for it reads "Ribh Considers Christian Love Insufficient." And yet the poem vibrates with a quality that is Christian in spite of the old pagan Ribh's ostensible attack upon Christianity. It is indeed a probing—deeper than many of our respectable Christian poems ever achieve—of what has been called the unconditional ground of our being:

> Why should I seek for love or study it?
> It is of God and passes human wit.
> I study hatred with great diligence,

For that's a passion in my own control,
A sort of besom that can clear the soul
Of everything that is not mind or sense.

Why do I hate man, woman or event?
That is a light my jealous soul has sent.
From terror and deception freed it can
Discover impurities, can show at last
How soul may walk when all such things are past,
How soul could walk before such things began.

Then my delivered soul herself shall learn
A darker knowledge and in hatred turn
From every thought of God mankind has had.
Thought is a garment and the soul's a bride
That cannot in that trash and tinsel hide:
Hatred of God may bring the soul to God.

At stroke of midnight soul cannot endure
A bodily or mental furniture.
What can she take until her Master give!
Where can she look until He make the show!
What can she know until He bid her know!
How can she live till in her blood He live.

I find in the later Yeats, by the way, a great deal of Nietzsche. The later Yeats rejoices in the celebration of man's sheer vitality and man's ability to do and to suffer. Nietzsche argued that in beauty "contrasts are overcome, the highest sign of power thus manifesting itself in the conquest of opposites." The artist, Nietzsche declared, creates out of joy and strength—not out of weakness—and the most convincing artists are precisely those "who make harmony ring out of every discord." The great artist is tested, Nietzsche felt, by the "extent to which he can acknowledge the terrible and questionable character of things," and still affirm the goodness of life.

These comments by Nietzsche apply beautifully to the magnificent poetry that Yeats wrote during the 'twenties and 'thirties. The Yeats of this period sees the typical tragic protagonist, a Hamlet or a Lear, as gay, "Gaiety transfiguring all that dread." Or again, as Yeats in 1936 looked out upon a world moving toward its second universal war, he could write:

> Irrational streams of blood are staining earth;
> Empedocles has thrown all things about;
> Hector is dead and there's a light in Troy;
> We that look on but laugh in tragic joy.

The later poetry of Yeats does indeed "make harmony ring out of every discord"—in its rapt exaltation deliberately introducing the discord sometimes so that the poet may display his ability to resolve it. In one of his earlier poems Yeats wrote of Dante that he "set his chisel to the hardest stone." At the end of his own career it is always to the hardest stone that Yeats sets his chisel.

You may well wonder how it can be claimed that this resemblance to Nietzsche argues for a Christian element in the poetry of Yeats, and yet I think that it can be so argued. Whatever Nietzsche's motives, we owe him something for helping us disentangle Christianity from timid bourgeois respectability. His indictment of Christianity as a slave morality has its value for those to whom true Christianity has meaning. Nietzsche's latest biographer and commentator says, "what [Nietzsche] denounces is not sincere Christianity, but insincere Christianity—those who are unchristian in their practice but nevertheless profess Christianity, as well as those who superficially seem Christian in their practice but whose motivation and state of mind is essentially unchristian." Be that as it may, Yeats goes far to restore to Christianity its proper dimension of awe and dread. For him it is not a passive thing but active and dynamic.

Perhaps this restoration of the dimension of awe is the most significant thing about Yeats' treatment of Christianity. He pushes away all the timid Victorian pieties and the soft pre-Raphaelite distortions and appeals again to the Christian force that displays itself in Byzantine art or in the European middle ages. And, most important of all, in either case Yeats takes the Christian symbols seriously by bringing them into direct relation to man's perennial problems. A good illustration can be found in the first of his "Two Songs for a Play." Yeats in the first stanza connects the Dionysian rites with the Christian mystery. The first stanza traces this continuity between Greek mystery religions and the Eucharist.

> I saw a staring virgin stand
> Where holy Dionysus died,
> And tear the heart out of his side,
> And lay the heart upon her hand
> And bear that beating heart away;
> And then did all the Muses sing
> Of Magnus Annus at the spring,
> As though God's death were but a play.

The second stanza suggests that the former cycle now repeats itself with Christian equivalents to those of Graeco-Roman paganism.

> Another Troy must rise and set,
> Another lineage feed the crow,
> Another Argo's painted prow
> Drive to a flashier bauble yet.
> The Roman Empire stood appalled:
> It dropped the reins of peace and war
> When that fierce virgin and her Star
> Out of the fabulous darkness called.

I would call your attention to the last lines. Here is no meek virgin of pre-Raphaelite art. She is a fierce virgin calling out of the fabulous darkness. She cries her challenge to the ordered power of the Roman empire, now at its zenith, and with her ringing cry she paralyzes it—"The Roman empire stood appalled."

One ought to observe in passing that the note sounded here is to be heard in certain other modern poets. Thus T. S. Eliot, for example, in his poem "Gerontion," sees Christ as a tiger—a powerful and terrible force. One remembers, too, in this connection that Henry Adams gives to the crucial chapter in *The Education* the significant title "The Virgin and the Dynamo."

The importance of religion is something which Yeats never doubts for a moment. As to which or what is the true religion, he is often in doubt and he plays with the notion that all religions are merely variants of one religion. But the abiding importance of religion itself never comes into question.

The "Two Songs from a Play" have to do with the shift from Graeco-classical civilization to Christian civilization. One of Yeats' most powerful poems, "The Second Coming," treats of the imminent shift over from Christian civilization to the civilization immediately ahead of us, one that will involve a reversal of all that has preceded it. This poem is probably one of the most celebrated of modern times. I should point out that since it was written in 1919 one could claim for it that it represents the poet as truly prophetic, looking ahead to Hitler, the Second World War, and the terrifying stresses of our own time, with a gaze far more discerning than that accorded to any social scientist or historian or economist.

THE SECOND COMING

Turning and turning in the widening gyre
The falcon cannot hear the falconer;
Things fall apart; the centre cannot hold;
Mere anarchy is loosed upon the world,
The blood-dimmed tide is loosed, and everywhere

The ceremony of innocence is drowned;
The best lack all conviction, while the worst
Are full of passionate intensity.

Surely some revelation is at hand;
Surely the Second Coming is at hand.
The Second Coming! Hardly are those words out
When a vast image out of *Spiritus Mundi*
Troubles my sight: somewhere in sands of the desert
A shape with lion body and the head of a man,
A gaze blank and pitiless as the sun,
Is moving its slow thighs, while all about it
Reel shadows of the indignant desert birds.
The darkness drops again; but now I know
That twenty centuries of stony sleep
Were vexed to nightmare by a rocking cradle,
And what rough beast, its hour come round at last,
Slouches towards Bethlehem to be born?

In this poem Yeats is using the Christian symbols such as the Second Coming and Bethlehem for his own special purposes. That, I readily grant. But we should not fail to notice that in using them for his own purposes, Yeats is nevertheless restoring them to urgency of meaning. Indeed for the Christian this is one of the most important things that Yeats does.

More than once, Yeats glances at the doctrine of the Incarnation, and reveals it as freshly meaningful. Consider in this connection his beautiful and tender poem, "A Prayer for My Son." I quote the last two stanzas. The "You" of the first line refers to God.

Though You can fashion everything
From nothing every day, and teach
The morning stars to sing,
You have lacked articulate speech
To tell Your simplest want, and known,

Wailing upon a woman's knee,
All of that worst ignominy
Of flesh and bone;

And when through all the town there ran
The servants of Your enemy,
A woman and a man,
Unless the Holy Writings lie,
Hurried through the smooth and rough
And through the fertile and waste,
Protecting, till the danger past,
With human love.

As for Yeats' personal beliefs as distinct from the dramatization of beliefs which fill his poetry—this, I repeat, is not easy to determine. The difficulty is in part that which dogs attempts to determine Shakespeare's personal beliefs. Like that great dramatist, Yeats throws himself into each new dramatic situation with sufficient ardor and conviction to give to each new poem his own personal energy, and thus to make it come alive. Thus he can write a brilliant celebration of natural beauty in his fine poem "Among School Children," but he can also in the very same period produce just as brilliant a celebration of intellectual beauty in "Sailing to Byzantium." It is idle to ask whether he personally preferred natural beauty to intellectual or vice versa.

So it is with reference to Yeats' Christian beliefs. I have quoted from "A Prayer for My Son," a poem which seems to take with utter seriousness the Incarnation as an event that actually happened. Yet in the same volume in which this poem appeared, another one, "Wisdom," asserts that the true faith was discovered only when the artist and the mythmaker "Amended what was told awry / By some peasant gospeller. . . ." This latter poem might be right out of late nineteenth-century German higher criticism—and ultimately, perhaps, that is its source. But Yeats' ability to adopt varying stances—what Yeats could have called his power of negative capability—is the source of Yeats' great strength as a poet.

On the positive side, Yeats was content to remain tentative and provisional. Throughout a lifetime he tirelessly pursued every path that might seem to lead to the ultimate truth. He was willing to try everything—the Hermetic sciences as revised by the adepts of the 'nineties, spirit mediums, hashish, table rapping—everything indeed from Hegel to Madame Blavatsky. In the light of some of Yeats' more bizarre and childish experiences with magic, the modern reader may have difficulty in taking Yeats' pursuit of truth with full seriousness. But Yeats was a more learned philosopher than he pretended to be, and some of his basic insights are profound.

Perhaps Yeats' most specific poetic statement as to why he felt unable to accept Christianity comes in a poem written in 1932, entitled "Vacillation." The poem is a suite of meditative lyrics on the subjects of joy, man's blessedness, and death. The seventh section is a dialogue between the soul and the heart; the eighth is addressed to the modern Christian mystic Baron von Hügel. I shall quote both sections, for both are relevant to our purpose here.

VII

The Soul. Seek out reality, leave things that seem.
The Heart. What, be a singer born and lack a theme?
The Soul. Isaiah's coal, what more can man desire?
The Heart. Struck dumb in the simplicity of fire!
The Soul. Look on that fire, salvation walks within.
The Heart. What theme had Homer but original sin?

VIII

Must we part, Von Hügel, though much alike, for we
Accept the miracles of the saints and honour sanctity?
The body of Saint Teresa lies undecayed in tomb,

Bathed in miraculous oil, sweet odours from it come,
Healing from its lettered slab. . . .
. . . I—though heart might find relief
Did I become a Christian man and choose for my belief
What seems most welcome in the tomb—play a predestined
part.
Homer is my example and his unchristened heart.
The lion and the honeycomb, what has Scripture said?
So get you gone, Von Hügel, though with blessings on
your head.

This theme—that the artist's role is analogous to that of the saint, that he renders to us something precious, not like the saint by renouncing the world, but by immersing himself in the world, even in the filth and horror of the world—this was a theme dear to Yeats, and constantly alluded to in one way or another. In *A Vision* he goes so far as to say that poets and artists like Baudelaire, Beardsley, and Dowson in their exploration of experience, actually come to suffer from forms of "emotional morbidity" which "others recognize as their own; as the Saint may take upon himself the physical diseases of others."

Yeats sent a first draft of "Vacillation" to a friend to whom he had previously written: "I begin to think I shall take to religion unless you save me from it." When the friend, eyeing the prospect rather askance, remarked that if Yeats got religion he would be "too great a bore," Yeats sent her the poem. He will not take to religion, this poem tells us. Isaiah's coal might strike him dumb—might so cauterize his lips with holiness that he could write no more poetry. The old poet will therefore persist with his "unchristened heart." Yet the parting with von Hügel is, it seems to me, a genuinely reluctant one, and the respect paid to sanctity is far more than merely nominal. In the letter itself Yeats tells his friend: "Yet I accept all the miracles. . . . Why should I doubt the tale that when St Theresa's tomb was opened in the middle of the nineteenth century the still undecayed body dripped with fragrant oil?" If in a passage such as this Yeats is candid in his denial of Christianity, yet the denial can give small comfort to the modern positivist or naturalist.

A fairly recent book on Yeats entitled *The Unicorn*, by Virginia Moore, devotes a whole chapter to the topic "Was Yeats a Christian?" Miss Moore strives valiantly to prove that Yeats was a Christian after all. She has to admit finally that he was heterodox, though "not perniciously so" and therefore not "heretical." Though I sympathize with Miss Moore's effort, I think that she forfeits, by the strained and forced interpretations to which she has to subject so much of the evidence, any chance of securing the neutral reader's conviction. In any case, the rather disappointingly meager conclusion at which she finally arrives can be reached by a more direct and plausible route. What we can say with confidence is that Yeats found his imagination gripped by the great Christian symbols, that he found his mind constantly engaged by the historical and doctrinal problems of Christianity, and that through a lifetime he struggled against the thin and vapid oversimplifications of pseudoscience and popular scientism. Most important of all for our purposes, he sought to dramatize the perennial human problems as living, imaginative realities. He posed the great questions, and it is these posings, these dramatizations, that are important for us—not Yeats' attempted solutions of these problems.

The last item in the volume of *Letters of W. B. Yeats*, edited by Allen Wade and published a few years ago, is addressed to Yeats' friend Lady Elizabeth Pelham:

> I know for certain [he writes to her] that my time will not be long. I have put away everything that can be put away that I may speak what I have to speak, and I find 'expression' is a part of 'study.' In two or three weeks—I am now idle that I may rest after writing

> much verse—I will begin to write my most fundamental thoughts and the arrangement of thought which I am convinced will complete my studies. I am happy, and I think full of an energy, of an energy I had despaired of. It seems to me that I have found what I wanted. When I try to put all into a phrase I say, 'Man can embody truth but he cannot know it.' I must embody it in the completion of my life. The abstract is not life and everywhere draws out its contradictions. You can refute Hegel but not the Saint or the Song of Sixpence.

Yeats' favorite collocation of saint and artist is thus hit upon once more at the very close of his life. One can refute the philosopher, but one cannot refute the truly well-made work of art. Yeats' own best poems are not subject to refutation. They embody truth even as the saint embodies truth. They embody whatever truth Yeats could find form for as a poet. My conviction is that in particular they yield to the Christian reader capable of dealing with them as works of art a great deal of truth—not as abstraction, not as "messages," not as sermons. I close with three examples. They vary in tone—from the extravagantly playful to the magnificently prophetic, but they all affirm with an incorrigible idealism the freedom of the soul and its responsibility. In each, Yeats refuses as poet to deal with the soul apart from the concreteness of the body.

My first example, Yeats' little poem "For Anne Gregory," is playful, but it more than glances at the doctrine of the Incarnation, and certainly it alludes to man's limitations as a mortal being who can know ultimate truth only through mediation—only, that is, through the imagination.

> 'Never shall a young man,
> Thrown into despair
> By those great honey-coloured
> Ramparts at your ear,
> Love you for yourself alone
> And not your yellow hair.'

'But I can get a hair-dye
And set such colour there,
Brown, or black, or carrot,
That young men in despair
May love me for myself alone
And not my yellow hair.'

'I heard an old religious man
But yesternight declare
That he had found a text to prove
That only God, my dear,
Could love you for yourself alone
And not your yellow hair.'

The last stanza is more than admirable fooling. Man is bounded by the world of the senses and presumes upon that fact at his peril. Otherwise, as Jacques Maritain would put it, man falls into "angelism."

The second poem that I would call to your attention is a short poem entitled "Death" which Yeats was moved to write at the political assassination of his friend Kevin O'Higgins. Before I present the poem it is proper to give a note on the first few lines. Yeats' contrast between man facing death and the animal facing death can be taken quite literally. An animal, all but lacking memory and quite without prevision of the future, cannot know what death is. The animal literally cannot know what is happening to it in the process of dying. (This is, I am convinced, the point that Keats makes in his "Ode to a Nightingale," in which he says to the nightingale "Thou wast not born for death, immortal bird.") Man, on the contrary, is sufficiently detached from nature to know that he will die. Unlike the nightingale, he is indeed born for death.

Nor dread nor hope attend
A dying animal;

A man awaits his end
Dreading and hoping all;
Many times he died,
Many times rose again.
A great man in his pride
Confronting murderous men
Casts derision upon
Supersession of breath;
He knows death to the bone—
Man has created death.

There is almost an exultant note in "man has created death." My preliminary comments on this little poem were designed to make us take this bold affirmation seriously—not at all to explain it away. It is a part of Yeats' almost belligerent idealistic credo, and Yeats sounds it again and again. He sounds it perhaps most impressively in one of the last poems that he wrote. The assertion of man's creation of death and thus his mastery of it is made in the second part of the poem, which I shall read.

UNDER BEN BULBEN

II

Many times man lives and dies
Between his two eternities,
That of race and that of soul,
And ancient Ireland knew it all.
Whether man die in his bed
Or the rifle knock him dead,
A brief parting from those dear
Is the worst man has to fear.
Though grave-diggers' toil is long,
Sharp their spades, their muscles strong,
They but thrust their buried men
Back in the human mind again.

The third section insists upon the violence necessary for any activity that is to have meaning. Even the wisest man experiences something like violence before he can accomplish his work.

III

You that Mitchel's prayer have heard,
'Send war in our time, O Lord!'
Know that when all words are said
And a man is fighting mad,
Something drops from eyes long blind.
He completes his partial mind,
For an instant stands at ease,
Laughs aloud, his heart at peace.
Even the wisest man grows tense
With some sort of violence
Before he can accomplish fate,
Know his work or choose his mate.

Here again Yeats stands close to Nietzsche. The true sense of completeness and wholeness does not come out of lassitude and timidity but is won from violent activity.

Section IV of the poem boldly states the case for the artist. In a very real sense the artist does "bring the soul of man to God." But our artist, Yeats, in the year before his death, is perfectly tough-minded and even casual about this. In celebrating the power of the artist to give us a supernatural vision he can bring together mathematics, the painter's pigments, and the gaping American tourist, on the Italian tour.

IV

Poet and sculptor, do the work,
Nor let the modish painter shirk
What his great forefathers did,
Bring the soul of man to God,
Make him fill the cradles right.

Measurement began our might:
Forms a stark Egyptian thought,
Forms that gentler Phidias wrought.
Michael Angelo left a proof
On the Sistine Chapel roof,
Where but half-awakened Adam
Can disturb globe-trotting Madam
Till her bowels are in heat,
Proof that there's a purpose set
Before the secret working mind:
Profane perfection of mankind.

Quattrocento put in paint
On backgrounds for a God or Saint
Gardens where a soul's at ease;
Where everything that meets the eye,
Flowers and grass and cloudless sky,
Resemble forms that are or seem
When sleepers wake and yet still dream,
And when it's vanished still declare,
With only bed and bedstead there,
That heavens had opened.

Section v of the aging poet's valedictory is addressed specifically to the poets and to the Irish poets. This part of the poem has provoked some readers to accuse Yeats of snobbery and parochial patriotism. But we should read it in context, and in the context it gives us Yeats still thundering against Whiggery and still celebrating in contrast to Whiggery the ideals of the peasant, the noble, and the saint.

v

Irish poets, learn your trade,
Sing whatever is well made,
Scorn the sort now growing up

All out of shape from toe to top,
Their unremembering hearts and heads
Base-born products of base beds.
Sing the peasantry, and then
Hard-riding country gentlemen,
The holiness of monks, and after
Porter-drinkers' randy laughter;
Sing the lords and ladies gay
That were beaten into the clay
Through seven heroic centuries;
Cast your mind on other days
That we in coming days may be
Still the indomitable Irishry.

The last section of the poem quite literally gives Yeats' directions for his burial, directions delayed by the state of the world at the time of his death in 1939 but since that time now actually carried out.

VI

Under bare Ben Bulben's head
In Drumcliff churchyard Yeats is laid.
An ancestor was rector there
Long years ago, a church stands near,
By the road an ancient cross.
No marble, no conventional phrase;
On limestone quarried near the spot
By his command these words are cut:
Cast a cold eye
On life, on death.
Horseman, pass by!

What Yeats' ecclesiastical ancestor, the rector of Drumcliff, would think of Yeats' poetry, and specifically, of this poem, I do not know, but I have no hesitation in saying what I believe we should think of it. It is mature poetry. It is brilliant and subtle poetry. Much of it is very great poetry. It asserts the dignity and power of the human spirit against the spiritual and intellectual corruption of our time. That is much to claim for it; that is all that I think necessary to claim for it.

5.

T. S. ELIOT

DISCOURSE TO THE GENTILES

T. S. Eliot is the most celebrated poet of our day. He is certainly the most distinguished Christian poet. Nowadays, and particularly in a group such as this, we are inclined to take his Christianity for granted. In this I think that there lies a real danger—not only that we shall distort and blur the finer outlines of his poetry; there is danger that we will distort and misapprehend the Christianity itself.

It may be salutary to remind ourselves that T. S. Eliot was not always a Christian and that his most famous poem was for long regarded as a distinctly un-Christian and even anti-Christian document. Burton Rascoe in his autobiographical *We Were Interrupted* writes: "T. S. Eliot's *The Waste Land* appeared in the November 1922 issue of the *Dial*, which was on the newsstands on October 26. I read the poem on that day and was so profoundly touched and shaken by it that, in recording my impression of it in my diary that night, I did not dare quite trust the adjectives I wished to use in praise of it for publication. I wrote that it was 'perhaps' the finest poem of the generation but conceded that it was 'the most significant in that it gives voice to the universal despair or resignation arising from the spiritual and economic consequences of the war, the cross-purposes of modern civilization . . .' et cetera."

A propos of such interpretations as this, Eliot was to remark in 1932: "when I wrote a poem called *The Waste Land* some of the more approving critics said that I had expressed the 'disillusionment of a generation,' which is nonsense. I may have expressed for them their own illusion of being disillusioned, but that did not form part of my intention."

Be that as it may, Burton Rascoe championed the poem *because* it was to his mind an expression of despair. It was Eliot's Christian position that Rascoe was later to find either boring or positively offensive. As he tells us: "I was to find neither [Eliot's] verse nor his prose to my liking after [*The Waste Land*.] From his embittered cynicism as an impious and talented young poet just out of Harvard, during his residence in England he leaped over the resplendent grand canyon of *The Waste Land* into Anglo-Catholicism and tory reactionarism. If he had found comfort therein for his troubled soul, I was glad for him, but thereafter I considered him an ally of the enemy."

If it is easy for us, with the benefit of hindsight, to view Rascoe's estimate of *The Waste Land* as rather absurd and to find his anti-clerical prejudices themselves parochial, we need to remember that pro-Christian prejudices can be limiting too. The spectacle of clergymen and vestrymen who had never in their lives paid any attention to modern literature trooping to the intellectual feast, now that they had heard that Eliot was a good churchman and an important poet—that spectacle has been sometimes amusing and a little pathetic. I don't mean to be stuffy about this. On one level this interest in Eliot is certainly to be welcomed, but in viewing the spectacle as I have had to on frequent occasions, one has so often sensed the fact that the churchly reader was in for disappointment and perhaps bewilderment—that Tennyson and Browning had scarcely prepared him for the idiom which he now had to master—that he could not realize that Eliot was presenting him with a whole new way of "seeing" reality and that his perhaps strained and tired eyes would require some time to adjust to this new angle of vision. Most of all, one knew that in so many such cases the reader, eager as he was for a detachable "message," would take away only what could be abstracted from the poetry, a rubric, a slogan, a generalization.

What I have just said may seem a curious introduction to a lecture on Eliot. Perhaps it seems rather pointedly intimidating: as if I were insisting on the formidable quality of Mr. Eliot—as if I were emphasizing his obscurity—as if I assumed that he could make sense only to the initiate. Such are the usual charges made against Eliot as a poet, and by what I have said, I may appear to you to be tacitly subscribing to them. That, however, is not my purpose. Rather, I should like to explain *why* such charges have been made and by explaining, free the poet from the usual implication of the charges—to wit, that Eliot is incurably snobbish and prefers to be misunderstood by all save a tiny cult.

The truth of the matter is that Eliot has from the beginning used a method of indirection. Even his avowedly Christian poetry is still indirect in this sense. *The Cocktail Party* will illustrate. Even in this play, done so late as 1950, the specifically Christian references are few. Is Sir Henry Harcourt-Reilly a psychiatrist? Or is he a priest? And the organization to which Alexander Gibbs refers—he has, he tells us, "connections—even in California"—is it the Church? We are never told. The play is insistently Christian, and yet it looks as if Eliot had quite deliberately played down the specific Christian references. I think that he has done so, here and in the rest of his poetry, but not for purposes of bafflement—not to mislead the reader. Such a strategy of indirection is enjoined upon him by the nature of his vision and the nature of the audience to which that vision is to be mediated.

Eliot's poetry, from the very beginning, is conceived in terms of the following problem: how is revealed truth to be mediated to the gentiles? How is that which is by definition ineffable to be translated into words, no direct transmission of the vision being possible. This problem engaged his attention simply as poet, long before he ever became a Christian poet. For the problem is that of the necessary indirection of poetry. Eliot would have encountered it early when he put himself to school to the French symbolists. Was it not Stéphane Mallarmé who said: "To name an object is to do away with three-quarters of the enjoyment of the poem which is derived from the satisfaction of guessing little by little: to suggest it, that is the illusion." In order to charm the imagination, one must "evoke an object little by little." R. G. Collingwood a few years ago put the case in a manner that strips it of any implications of art for art's sake: "A genuine poet, in his moments of genuine poetry, never mentions by name the emotions he is expressing." And he goes on to indicate why. "The reason why description, so far from helping expression, actually damages it, is that description generalizes. To describe a thing is to call it a thing of such and such a kind: to bring it under a conception, to classify it. Expression, on the contrary, individualizes. . . . The poet, therefore, in proportion as he understands his business, gets as far away as possible from merely labelling his emotions as instances of this or that general kind, and takes enormous pains to individualize them by expressing them in terms which reveal their difference from any other emotion of the same sort."

The genuine poet is of course always concerned with a specific and concrete and individual experience; the undifferentiated generalization, the cliché, the stereotype—these are symptoms of his failure—of the kind of falsification that pertains peculiarly to art. The poet *must* be indirect, and as a consequence he always has to say to his audience: he that hath ears to hear, let him hear. Even if he yearns for the largest audience possible—and what writer does not?—he still cannot supply the ears for his audience. He can do no more than to try by various devices—intimation, dramatic shock, change of tone, ironic confrontation, and all the other rhetorical and poetic devices—to wheedle or bludgeon his audience into attending to what he has to say and, by bringing their faculties to alertness, putting themselves in a position to apprehend his meaning. But the apprehension has to be performed by the audience—it cannot be delegated to anyone else—not even assumed by the poet himself. In short, the poet can write his poem for us; he cannot read it for us.

So much for the general problem of artistic indirection. For the Christian poet writing in and for a thoroughly secular society, the claims of a method of indirection become much more urgent. Not only do the Christian symbols that most people would expect the poet to use fail to convey his meaning; they may actively distort his meaning. What I have in mind is something analogous to what Coleridge describes in talking of Wordsworth's part in their joint book *Lyrical Ballads*. Wordsworth, Coleridge tells us, undertook to awaken "the mind's attention from the lethargy of custom," to apprehend the wonders of the world, to apprehend what is truly "an inexhaustible treasure" but a treasure for which, because of "the film of Familiarity and selfish solicitude we have eyes, yet see not, ears that hear not, and hearts that neither feel nor understand." But the Christian symbols are obscured by more than a "film of familiarity." For the men of our time the Christian symbols have often been darkened and distorted, in some cases almost beyond recognition—and not only for the non-Christian but, one is tempted to say, for the Christian as well. The poet's task is not only to find new symbols for the central experiences but to reconstitute the old symbols, reclaiming them, redeeming them, setting them in contexts which will force us once again to confront their Christian meanings.

The characters in Eliot's own poems and plays are thoroughly involved in this problem of expression. Listen to Sweeney in Eliot's *Fragment of an Agon* as, facing his group of raffish friends, he concludes his story about a man he knew once who "did a girl in."

> For when you're alone
> When you're alone like he was alone
> You're either or neither
> I tell you again it dont apply
> Death or life or life or death
> Death is life and life is death
> I gotta use words when I talk to you
> But if you understand or if you dont
> That's nothing to me and nothing to you.

One must use words: one cannot simply communicate the raw emotion—the naked vision. Sweeney's creator knows that full well. Here he himself speaks to the subject in "East Coker":

> So here I am, in the middle way, having had twenty years—
> Twenty years largely wasted, the years of *l'entre deux guerres*—
> Trying to learn to use words, and every attempt
> Is a wholly new start, and a different kind of failure
> Because one has only learnt to get the better of words
> For the thing one no longer has to say, or the way in which
> One is no longer disposed to say it.

For a more specific instance of the problem of stating the Christian experience, however, let us listen to one of Eliot's characters in *The Cocktail Party*. Here is Celia in the office of Sir Henry Harcourt-Reilly preparing to have her "illness" diagnosed.

Celia: Well, I can't pretend that my trouble is interesting;
 But I shan't begin that way. I feel perfectly well.
 I could lead an active life—if there's anything to work for;
 I don't imagine that I am being persecuted;
 I don't hear any voices, I have no delusions—
 Except that the world I live in seems all a delusion!
 But oughtn't I first to tell you the circumstances?
 I'd forgotten that you know nothing about me;
 And with what I've been going through, these last weeks,
 I somehow took it for granted that I needn't explain myself.
Reilly: I know quite enough about you for the moment:
 Try first to describe your present state of mind.
Celia: Well, there are two things I can't understand,
 Which you might consider symptoms. But first I must tell you
 That I should really *like* to think there's something
  wrong with me—
 Because, if there isn't, then there's something wrong,
 Or at least, very different from what it seemed to be,
 With the world itself—and that's much more frightening!
 That would be terrible. So I'd rather believe
 There is something wrong with me, that could be put right.

The two things that Celia says she cannot understand are first "An awareness of solitude"—she realizes now that actually she has always been alone; and second, an awareness of sin. Celia almost blushes to confess the latter fact:

 It sounds ridiculous—but the only word for it
 That I can find, is a sense of sin.
Reilly: You suffer from a sense of sin, Miss Coplestone?
 This is most unusual.

What makes the matter quite unaccountable is the fact that her upbringing was, as she puts it,

> pretty conventional—
> I had always been taught to disbelieve in sin.
> Oh, I don't mean that it was ever mentioned!
> But anything wrong, from our point of view,
> Was either bad form, or was psychological.

Celia is quite aware of the old-fashioned absurdity of the term she is using. She is just as much aware of it as the young woman in the London or New York theater who was there to view the performance of the play, a young woman who like Celia had been to the best schools and had read the prescribed books and was *au courant* with the newest intellectual fashions.

Harry, the tormented hero of Eliot's *The Family Reunion*, can be regarded as at some points a preliminary study of Celia. Harry's discovery of sin, like Celia's, finds him almost incredulous and certainly well aware of what the other members of his family will think of his odd aberration. He asks them:

> You've been holding a meeting—the usual family inquest
> On the characters of all the junior members?
> Or engaged in predicting the minor event,
> Engaged in foreseeing the minor disaster?
> You go on trying to think of each thing separately,
> Making small things important, so that everything
> May be unimportant, a slight deviation
> From some imaginary course that life ought to take,
> That you call normal. What you call the normal
> Is merely the unreal and the unimportant.
> I was like that in a way, so long as I could think
> Even of my own life as an isolated ruin,
> A casual bit of waste in an orderly universe.

> But it begins to seem just part of some huge disaster,
> Some monstrous mistake and aberration
> Of all men, of the world, which I cannot put in order.

The characters in Eliot who make this discovery of evil and find it an objective thing actually there in the external world, not a subjective delusion, recover their freedom. They experience a sense of release. But they have great difficulty in communicating the meaning of the experience to others. As Harry says

> . . . when one has just recovered sanity,
> And not yet assured in possession, that is when
> One begins to seem the maddest to other people.

To most of his family Harry does seem quite mad. But the failure of communication in this instance goes further still. For most readers Eliot himself is adjudged to have failed: the experience with which the play evidently concerns itself is not conveyed. (Eliot himself, by the by, with characteristic candor has cheerfully acknowledged the failure.)

Even the people who find *The Cocktail Party* on the whole an interesting and successful play find it difficult to accept Celia as a believable character. I myself find Celia thoroughly credible, but I record the fact that many readers—including readers disposed to admire Eliot—do not. They do not, I think, simply because they cannot comprehend what it feels like to have a sense of sin or to wish to make atonement or to feel abnegation.

The modern reader has been taught to explain away all these things as abnormalities. This fact will help to account for Eliot's avoiding Christian terms and Christian symbols. One notices also that even in the avowedly Christian works, Eliot shows himself to be constantly aware of this problem of modern incomprehension. For example in *Murder in the Cathedral* he has to face the problem of presenting a martyrdom to a world which has reduced all such self-sacrificial action to a psychic abnormality —the expression of a martyr complex. Eliot's attempted solution is interesting and almost desperate. The fourth of the tempters who come to Thomas plainly prophesies what is to occur in subsequent history: the shrine of St. Thomas will be pillaged, the gold spent, the jewels bestowed upon whores. But worse still is to come:

> When miracles cease, and the faithful desert you,
> And men shall only do their best to forget you.
> And later is worse, when men will not hate you
> Enough to defame or to execrate you,
> But pondering the qualities that you lacked
> Will only try to find the historical fact.
> When men shall declare that there was no mystery
> About this man who played a certain part in history.

A little later in the play Thomas, in the long speech which closes the first part of the play, suddenly breaks out of the twelfth-century dramatic situation and addresses himself to us, the modern readers:

> I know
> What yet remains to show you of my history
> Will seem to most of you at best futility,
> Senseless self-slaughter of a lunatic,
> Arrogant passion of a fanatic.
> I know that history at all times draws
> The strangest consequence from remotest cause.
> But for every evil, every sacrilege,
> Crime, wrong, oppression and the axe's edge,
> Indifference, exploitation, you, and you,
> And you, must all be punished. So must you.

> I shall no longer act or suffer, to the sword's end.
> Now my good Angel, whom God appoints
> To be my guardian, hover over the swords' points.

This is the same kind of artistic violence that Eliot had used many years before in *The Waste Land* where the Protagonist, as Part I closes, suddenly thrusts his hand clear through the dramatic envelope of the poem to pluck the sleeve of the reader:

> You! hypocrite lecteur!—mon semblable,—mon frère!

Again, Eliot has been just as daringly violent in having the four knights, after murdering Thomas, speak in political journalese just as if they stood upon the husting in a modern British election. For example, the fourth knight closes his speech as follows:

> [Becket] used every means of provocation; from his conduct, step by step, there can be no inference except that he had determined upon a death by martyrdom. This man, formerly a great public servant, had become a wrecker. Even at the last, he could have given us reason: you have seen how he evaded our questions. And when he had deliberately exasperated us beyond human endurance, he could still have easily escaped; he could have kept himself from us long enough to allow our righteous anger to cool. That was just what he did not wish to happen; he insisted, while we were still inflamed with wrath, that the doors should be opened. Need I say more? I think, with these facts before you, you will unhesitatingly render a verdict of Suicide while of Unsound Mind. It is the only charitable verdict you can give, upon one who was, after all, a great man.

I am happy to call attention to Eliot's use of such violent techniques, for one misunderstands the problem that I have been trying to put to you if he takes Eliot to be attempting quietly to insinuate Christian doctrine with a gentle and politic duplicity. It is not a question of sugar-coating a pill or slipping up on the blind side of the reader. Shock technique may be one of the necessary methods, for the problem is not finally a problem of rhetoric—that is, of persuading a particular audience—so much as it is a problem of poetic strategy: that is, Eliot himself, in order to present his insights honestly and fairly, must take account of the climate of opinion in which he as well as his audience lives.

Let me sum up at this point by saying that Eliot refuses to isolate his Christian materials: their very expression has to be related to the neutral or hostile environment of our day. It is not a matter of countering the "sales resistance" of the average reader: it is a problem of the poet's own integrity of presentation.

A closely related aspect of this refusal to simplify is Eliot's practice of using one and the same image to represent Christian and non-Christian elements. To take a simple instance, "rock" is part of the desert imagery and in poems like *The Waste Land* and *The Hollow Men* is used, along with the sand and the cactus imagery to suggest the spiritual barrenness of our time. Yet "rock" also stands in Eliot's poetry for stability and the certainty of faith. Even in *The Waste Land*, the protagonist hears:

> Come in under the shadow of this red rock. . . .

And in Eliot's pageant play entitled *The Rock* the character who speaks the word of God, "the God-shaken in whom is the truth inborn," actually bears the name of "The Rock."

Again, since *light* in Eliot's poetry, as in the general Christian tradition as represented by Dante and Milton, is a symbol for the divine, one expects darkness to represent the opposite of the divine, but darkness in Eliot's poetry is frequently used to represent not spiritual death but the way into spiritual life. For example, in *Four Quartets*, the speaker says:

I said to my soul, be still, and let the dark come upon you
Which shall be the darkness of God.

The symbol of the spiritual sterility of the temporal world in this poem is not darkness but "dim light." Our life in this world represents

neither daylight
Investing form with lucid stillness
Turning shadow into transient beauty
With slow rotation suggesting permanence
Nor darkness to purify the soul
Emptying the sensual with deprivation
Cleansing affection from the temporal.
Neither plenitude nor vacancy.

Again the false appearance of springtime that a winter day may show is used by Eliot with varying symbolic meaning.

Snow in the branches
Shall float as sweet as blossoms. Ice along the ditches
Mirror the sunlight.

This description of the wintertime spring is spoken by the First Tempter who visits Thomas in *Murder in the Cathedral*. One is inclined to view this false semblance of spring in the cold barren time of the year as perfectly suited to the tempter's specious promises. Accordingly, the reader may be shocked to find in the opening section of "Little Gidding" this same spring-in-winter, described in much the same way but used for an entirely different purpose. In this fourth section of the *Quartets* the season so described becomes a symbol of the eternal—a glimpse of the timeless world caught momentarily in the world of time.

> Midwinter spring is its own season
> Sempiternal though sodden towards sundown,
> Suspended in time, between pole and tropic.
> When the short day is brightest, with frost and fire,
> The brief sun flames the ice, on pond and ditches,
> In windless cold that is the heart's heat,
> Reflecting in a watery mirror
> A glare that is blindness in the early afternoon.
> And glow more intense than blaze of branch, or brazier,
> Stirs the dumb spirit: no wind, but pentecostal fire
> In the dark time of the year. Between melting and freezing
> The soul's sap quivers. There is no earth smell
> Or smell of living thing. This is the spring time
> But not in time's covenant. Now the hedgerow
> Is blanched for an hour with transitory blossom
> Of snow, a bloom more sudden
> Than that of summer, neither budding nor fading,
> Not in the scheme of generation.
> Where is the summer, the unimaginable
> Zero summer?

In viewing these instances of shifting meaning and double meaning—and they are thoroughly typical of Eliot's practice—we shall utterly mistake the point if we assume that they reveal carelessness or considered duplicity. They make the poetry more difficult to read, to be sure; but that difficulty has not been sought by Eliot. The truth of the matter is that it could not be avoided—it could not be avoided, that is, if the poet were to be true to his vision and true to the circumstances under which that vision was vouchsafed. For the very point about the modern world is that the old landmarks are gone—that we cannot afford to trust to stereotypes—that one and the same object changes meaning in being moved from one spiritual context to another. Our own society which tends to assign fixed meanings and to adhere to them mechanically—our society which dreads mystery and is fearful of paradoxes—our own society in particular has to be taught to look beneath surface appearances and to regard things from shifting points if it is to *see* anything to the purpose at all.

In a lecture upon Matthew Arnold, delivered at Harvard in 1933 and subsequently published in *The Use of Poetry*, Eliot was drawn to comment upon Arnold's remark, made with reference to Robert Burns, that "no one can deny that it is of advantage to a poet to deal with a beautiful world." Eliot says:

> this remark strikes me as betraying a limitation. It is an advantage to mankind in general to live in a beautiful world; that no one can doubt. But for the poet is it so important? We mean all sorts of things, I know, by Beauty. But the essential advantage for a poet is not to have a beautiful world with which to deal: it is to be able to see beneath both beauty and ugliness; to see the boredom, and the horror, and the glory.
>
> The vision of the horror and the glory was denied to Arnold, but he knew something of the boredom.

I am not the first to connect these observations with Eliot's own performance; but I shall go on to use them again. They apply so well to Eliot's own poetry that they may well furnish a framework for what I have to say in the remainder of this lecture.

Eliot's world, we may begin by observing, is not a beautiful world. It is in large part an urban world where one hears "rattling plates in basement kitchens," where, with morning, hands raise "dingy shades / In a thousand furnished rooms," where the "winter evening settles down / With smell of steaks in passageways" or where "a gusty shower wraps / The grimy scraps / Of withered leaves about your feet / And newspapers from vacant lots."

But whether in its more sordid slums or in the drawing rooms of the upper classes "where the women come and go / Talking of Michelangelo," it is a world that suffers from inertia and boredom. When evening "quickens faintly in the street," it wakens "the appetites of life in some" but to others evening simply brings "the *Boston Evening Transcript.*" It is a world that is not only bored but neurasthenic. In *The Waste Land* the lady in the rich room shivers in her isolation:

> Under the firelight, under the brush, her hair
> Spread out in fiery points
> Glowed into words, then would be savagely still.
>
> "My nerves are bad to-night. Yes, bad. Stay with me.
> "Speak to me. Why do you never speak. Speak.
> "What are you thinking of? What thinking? What?
> "I never know what you are thinking. Think."

But her state of nerves is linked to her boredom—her having lost any sense of meaning or direction. She bursts out with

> "What shall I do now? What shall I do?
> "I shall rush out as I am, and walk the street
> "With my hair down, so. What shall we do to-morrow?
> "What shall we ever do?"
> The hot water at ten.
> And if it rains, a closed car at four.
> And we shall play a game of chess,
> Pressing lidless eyes and waiting for a knock upon the door.

One of the primary symbols that Eliot uses by which to depict a pointless and meaningless activity is that of the wheel. The image occurs constantly in Eliot's poetry and in a dozen variants. One of the most obvious instances is that which occurs in the first chorus of *The Rock.*

> The Eagle soars in the summit of Heaven,
> The Hunter with his dogs pursues his circuit.

O perpetual revolution of configured stars,
O perpetual recurrence of determined seasons,
O world of spring and autumn, birth and dying!
The endless cycle of idea and action,
Endless invention, endless experiment,
Brings knowledge of motion, but not of stillness;
Knowledge of speech, but not of silence;
Knowledge of words, and ignorance of the Word.
All our knowledge brings us nearer to our ignorance,
All our ignorance brings us nearer to death,
But nearness to death no nearer to GOD.
Where is the Life we have lost in living?
Where is the wisdom we have lost in knowledge?
Where is the knowledge we have lost in information?
The cycles of Heaven in twenty centuries
Bring us farther from GOD and nearer to the Dust.

Madame Sosostris, the fortune teller in *The Waste Land* sees "crowds of people, walking in a ring," and the Hollow Men "Under the twinkle of a fading star" go round and round "the prickly pear / At five o'clock in the morning." Seen merely historically, all human activity appears to be merely cyclic, a repetition of habitual action. Thus in "East Coker" the vision of medieval peasantry takes the form of dancing in a ring.

Round and round the fire
Leaping through the flames, or joined in circles,
Rustically solemn or in rustic laughter
Lifting heavy feet in clumsy shoes,
Earth feet, loam feet, lifted in country mirth
Mirth of those long since under earth
Nourishing the corn. Keeping time,
Keeping the rhythm in their dancing
As in their living in the living seasons
The time of the seasons and the constellations

> The time of milking and the time of harvest
> The time of the coupling of man and woman
> And that of beasts. Feet rising and falling.
> Eating and drinking. Dung and death.

But this turning movement, viewed more somberly, conceived as a meaningless whirling motion, acquires the terror of a nightmare. Here follows a vision of numbed modern man, half dazed by the traffic of the secular world.

> Only a flicker
> Over the strained time-ridden faces
> Distracted from distraction by distraction
> Filled with fancies and empty of meaning
> Tumid apathy with no concentration
> Men and bits of paper, whirled by the cold wind
> That blows before and after time,
> Wind in and out of unwholesome lungs
> Time before and time after.

Few men, it goes without saying, attain to the vision of horror. They are whirled by the cold wind without realizing that they are whirled. They feel no more than a vague unease, or are able to shake off that unease, "Distracted from distraction by distraction." They may even have the illusion that they are turning the wheel upon which they turn. This is the situation upon which Thomas à Becket comments in his reply to the First Tempter:

> We do not know very much of the future
> Except that from generation to generation
> The same things happen again and again.
> Men learn little from others' experience.
> But in the life of one man, never
> The same time returns. Sever
> The cord, shed the scale. Only
> The fool, fixed in his folly, may think
> He can turn the wheel on which he turns.

Most of us, however, *are* either guilty of such folly or are else too numbed to notice what is happening—or too well brought up in secularist doctrine to do more than acquiesce

> while the world moves
> In appetency, on its metalled ways
> Of time past and time future.

That is why it will be difficult for the poet to give us his vision of the horror.

What are some of the ways in which Eliot has tried to convey this sense of the horror? There are many, but we may profitably begin with *The Family Reunion*, which, whether or not it is itself successful, certainly constitutes one of the best glosses upon Eliot's other work. Here is Harry, the hero of the play, trying to tell his Aunt Agatha about the horror as he has experienced it.

> At the beginning, eight years ago,
> I felt, at first, that sense of separation,
> Of isolation unredeemable, irrevocable—
> It's eternal, or gives a knowledge of eternity,
> Because it feels eternal while it lasts. That is one hell.
> Then the numbness came to cover it—that is another—
> That was the second hell of not being there,
> The degradation of being parted from my self,
> From the self which persisted only as an eye, seeing.

And a little later Harry tries once more to describe it:

> In and out, in an endless drift
> Of shrieking forms in a circular desert
> Weaving with contagion of putrescent embraces
> On dissolving bone. In and out, the movement
> Until the chain broke, and I was left
> Under the single eye above the desert.

But the most powerful and successful of these evocations of the abyss is that which occurs in *Murder in the Cathedral.* The chorus of Old Women of Canterbury are like most of us. They are not happy, but they fear the "disturbance of the quiet seasons." They want nothing to happen. They dread the decisive action, for it is a "fear like birth and death" and, like the people of *The Waste Land,* they shrink from rebirth. Their disquieting foreboding rises to a crescendo with the appearance of the knights and their sense that Thomas' martyrdom is imminent.

I have smelt them, the death-bringers, senses are quickened
By subtile forebodings; I have heard
Fluting in the nighttime, fluting and owls, have seen at noon
Scaly wings slanting over, huge and ridiculous. I have tasted
The savour of putrid flesh in the spoon. I have felt
The heaving of earth at nightfall, restless, absurd. I have heard
Laughter in the noises of beasts that make strange noises:
  jackal, jackass, jackdaw; the scurrying noise of mouse and jerboa;
  the laugh of the loon, the lunatic bird. I have seen
Grey necks twisting, rat tails twining, in the thick light of dawn.
  I have eaten
Smooth creatures still living, with the strong salt taste of living
  things under sea; I have tasted
The living lobster, the crab, the oyster, the whelk and the prawn;
  and they live and spawn in my bowels, and my bowels dissolve
  in the light of dawn. I have smelt
Death in the rose, death in the hollyhock, sweet pea, hyacinth,
  primrose and cowslip.

. . . I have smelt
Corruption in the dish, incense in the latrine, the sewer in the
  incense, the smell of sweet soap in the woodpath, a hellish sweet
  scent in the woodpath, while the ground heaved. I have seen
Rings of light coiling downwards, leading
To the horror of the ape.

It is an inverted and monstrous world that swims before their senses, brilliantly presented so as to suggest a kind of moral giddiness. The animal imagery and the imagery of smell are so used as to define the special kind of waking nightmare that confronts them. But it is only after this sense of topsy-turvy upheaval passes that they have their vision of the abyss—the ultimate nothingness. It is presented with a dry and terrifying clarity.

> The agents of hell disappear, the human, they shrink and dissolve
> Into dust on the wind, forgotten, unmemorable; only is here
> The white flat face of Death, God's silent servant,
> And behind the face of Death the Judgement
> And behind the Judgement the Void, more horrid than active
> shapes of hell;
> Emptiness, absence, separation from God;
> The horror of the effortless journey, to the empty land
> Which is no land, only emptiness, absence, the Void,
> Where those who were men can no longer turn the mind
> To distraction, delusion, escape into dream, pretence,
> Where the soul is no longer deceived, for there are no objects,
> no tones,
> No colours, no forms to distract, to divert the soul
> From seeing itself, foully united forever, nothing with nothing,
> Not what we call death, but what beyond death is not death,
> We fear, we fear.

I am told that Eliot himself once had a vision of the abyss—the middle of a London street opened before his eyes—the sort of experience that one of the minor characters in *The Family Reunion* imagines happening. That character says

> And now I don't feel safe. As if the earth should open
> Right to the centre, as I was about to cross Pall Mall.

The experience of the abyss does, as Harry has said, give "a knowledge of eternity." That knowledge, of course, Eliot has also tried to give more positively. Yet it is apparently always more difficult to write of heaven than of hell. It is most difficult of all to do so in an age which has good reason to find in hell at least a lively metaphor for certain conditions with which it is all too familiar but can see no point at all in the concept of heaven. Here then Eliot's special problem of presentation comes to a head. His later poetry may be regarded as a sustained attempt to suggest how we, immersed in the world of time as we are, can win to any kind of comprehension of the timeless.

This problem, of course, has haunted Eliot from the beginning. In *The Waste Land*, for example, the protagonist has an experience that seems to take him out of the realm of time. He remembers the moment with the girl in the hyacinth garden:

> —Yet when we came back, late, from the Hyacinth garden,
> Your arms full, and your hair wet, I could not
> Speak, and my eyes failed, I was neither
> Living nor dead, and I knew nothing,
> Looking into the heart of light, the silence.

But for all its poignance the experience is abortive. Into the speaker's mind there comes, to serve as somber and chilling commentary upon the experience, the line from Wagner's *Tristan und Isolde*, "Oed' und leer das Meer," empty and wide the sea.

Four Quartets will provide the clearest instances of this experience of apprehending eternity—"The point of intersection of the timeless / With time." For most of us, the speaker in "The Dry Salvages" is honest enough to say, there are "only hints and guesses, / Hints followed by guesses." Few of us are saints. Involved in the world of time, distracted by the creatures of time, we are vouchsafed only intimations, something half-glimpsed—

out of the tail of the eye, something discerned on the margin of vision—which vanishes when we try to focus our attention upon it. The speaker himself in the *Quartets* makes no pretense to the saint's vocation. He obviously includes himself among the "us" for whom

> there is only the unattended
> Moment, the moment in and out of time,
> The distraction fit, lost in a shaft of sunlight,
> The wild thyme unseen, or the winter lightning
> Or the waterfall, or music heard so deeply
> That it is not heard at all, but you are the music
> While the music lasts.

Yet some of these elusive images of sight and sound and smell are brilliantly suggestive and convey something of what it must feel like to have the experience. As we embark upon a consideration of some of those to be found in the *Quartets* I ask you to observe how completely honest the poet is. The fact of self-deception is not only granted—it is foreseen. The poet is cautious not to claim more than he can properly claim.

I cite first the experience of the rose-garden from the first of the *Quartets*, "Burnt Norton." Earlier, in Part II of *Ash Wednesday*, Eliot has inserted a poem celebrating under the image of the rose garden that love that is not desire manifesting itself in movement, but the love that "is itself unmoving / Only the cause and end of movement."

> The single Rose
> Is now the Garden
> Where all loves end
> Terminate torment
> Of love unsatisfied
> The greater torment

Of love satisfied
End of the endless
Journey to no end
Conclusion of all that
Is inconclusible
Speech without word and
Word of no speech
Grace to the Mother
For the Garden
Where all love ends.

This beautiful lyric gathers up and reconciles a number of Eliot's preoccupations. But it is in the mode of aspiration. In "Burnt Norton" the experience of the eternal touches our mundane life. We have a man walking into an actual earthly garden and there receiving, within the world of the senses, a hint of an order that transcends the sensual world.

Other echoes
Inhabit the garden. Shall we follow?
Quick, said the bird, find them, find them,
Round the corner. Through the first gate,
Into our first world, shall we follow
The deception of the thrush? Into our first world.
There they were, dignified, invisible,
Moving without pressure, over the dead leaves,
In the autumn heat, through the vibrant air,
And the bird called, in response to
The unheard music hidden in the shrubbery,
And the unseen eyebeam crossed, for the roses
Had the look of flowers that are looked at.
There they were as our guests, accepted and accepting.
So we moved, and they, in a formal pattern,
Along the empty alley, into the box circle,
To look down into the drained pool.

Dry the pool, dry concrete, brown edged,
And the pool was filled with water out of sunlight,
And the lotos rose, quietly, quietly,
The surface glittered out of heart of light,
And they were behind us, reflected in the pool.
Then a cloud passed, and the pool was empty.
Go, said the bird, for the leaves were full of children,
Hidden excitedly, containing laughter.
Go, go, go, said the bird: human kind
Cannot bear very much reality.
Time past and time future
What might have been and what has been
Point to one end, which is always present.

Human kind "cannot bear very much reality." And this fact is a boon as well as a curse. As the poet goes on to say further on in this poem

. . . the enchainment of past and future
Woven in the weakness of the changing body,
Protects mankind from heaven and damnation
Which flesh cannot endure.

Something further of what the poem means here is lighted up by the lines that immediately follow:

Time past and time future
Allow but a little consciousness.
To be conscious is not to be in time.

In *The Family Reunion*, on learning that his brother has been in a motor accident and has suffered a concussion, Harry remarks:

A minor trouble like a concussion
Cannot make very much difference to John.

A brief vacation from the kind of consciousness
That John enjoys, can't make very much difference
To him or to anyone else. If he was ever really conscious,
I should be glad for him to have a breathing spell.

Violet promptly accuses her nephew of being callous; and perhaps he is. That matter, however, has nothing to do with the present point, which is this: as mortal creatures we necessarily live in our creaturely world of time, and we pierce through this world, not only with great difficulty, if at all, but at our peril. That is one point. But there is another connected with this insight that "To be conscious is not to be in time": for us creatures of time, such moments of enlarged consciousness, such glimpses of the eternal as we may have, can be recalled and held on to only in the sequence of time. Thus

only in time can the moment in the rose-garden,
The moment in the arbour where the rain beat,
The moment in the draughty church at smokefall
Be remembered; involved with past and future.
Only through time time is conquered.

Earlier I called attention to Eliot's use of the image of the wheel as a symbol for the cycle of time and for merely mechanical, meaningless activity. The wheel image is, however, made to yield an image of the eternal. Every wheel implies a center, a mathematical point which itself does not alter position though such a central point is necessary if there is to be any rotation at all. The world of time is represented by the turning rim of the wheel; eternity is the unmoving center necessarily implied by the movement of time.

Eliot first used this symbolism in the fifth section of *Ash Wednesday* in a passage in which the speaker meditates on the Word of God, the Logos. Even though unheard, the Logos, he reflects, still exists, is still the Word; and the poet goes on to say

And the light shone in darkness and
Against the Word the unstilled world still whirled
About the centre of the silent Word.

But in the first of the *Four Quartets* this symbolism of the still center receives great elaboration:

At the still point of the turning world. Neither flesh nor fleshless;
Neither from nor towards; at the still point, there the dance is,
But neither arrest nor movement. And do not call it fixity,
Where past and future are gathered. Neither movement from nor
  towards,
Neither ascent nor decline. Except for the point, the still point,
There would be no dance, and there is only the dance.
I can only say, *there* we have been: but I cannot say where.
And I cannot say, how long, for that is to place it in time.

The passages that I have read from *Four Quartets* do not exhaust the analogies which the poet sets forth in his various attempts to intimate to us what his apprehension of the timeless is like. There is the sense of completeness and fulfilment, but along with these the sense of release from action and suffering. The experience is analogous to the motion that one experiences in a dance where movement and pattern become one, or it is like a finely conceived vase or Chinese jar, so shaped that though in fact static, it seems to move in its stillness like a dynamic thing. The sense of harmony is analogous again to what one finds in a finely wrought poem, where each part implies the whole of which it is a part, so that truly the end of the poem is implicit in the very beginning of the poem. But surely I shall do best to quote one of the passages in which the poet says these things for himself in his own way, allowing my own comments to serve simply as a preliminary gloss upon the passage:

> Words move, music moves
> Only in time; but that which is only living
> Can only die. Words, after speech, reach
> Into the silence. Only by the form, the pattern,
> Can words or music reach
> The stillness, as a Chinese jar still
> Moves perpetually in its stillness.
> Not the stillness of the violin, while the note lasts,
> Not that only, but the co-existence,
> Or say that the end precedes the beginning,
> And the end and the beginning were always there
> Before the beginning and after the end.
> And all is always now.

I have remarked more than once in this paper on the modesty of the poet, on what has to be termed his essential humility:

> to apprehend
> The point of intersection of the timeless
> With time, is an occupation for the saint—
> No occupation either, but something given
> And taken, in a lifetime's death in love,
> Ardour and selflessness and self-surrender.

For the rest of us, the poet says in a passage that I have quoted earlier, there are only the hints and guesses:

> and the rest
> Is prayer, observance, discipline, thought and action.
> The hint half guessed, the gift half understood, is Incarnation.

I want to emphasize this last line, for it is crucial. Eliot nowhere tries to bypass man's mortal imagination. In this life we cannot see face to face but only as in a mirror darkly. The poet must make use of analogies. Man cannot transcend the life of the senses by his own power. In an interesting volume of essays entitled *The Forlorn Demon* Allen Tate has written upon Edgar Allan Poe's yearning after what Tate calls the "angelic imagination," and Tate contrasts with this Dante's constant respect for man's finite condition and Dante's reliance upon analogy as the mode that man's finitude enjoins upon him. Tate writes:

"The human intellect cannot reach God as essence; only God as analogy. Analogy to what? Plainly analogy to the natural world; for there is nothing in the intellect that has not previously reached it through the senses. Had Dante arrived at the vision of God by way of sense? We must answer yes, because Dante's Triune Circle is light, which the finite intelligence can see only in what has already been seen by means of it. But Poe's center is that place—to use Dante's great figure—"where the sun is silent." Since he refuses to see nature, he is doomed to see nothing. He has overleaped and cheated the condition of man. The reach of our imaginative enlargement is perhaps no longer than the ladder of analogy, at the top of which we may see all, if we still wish to *see* anything, that we have brought up with us from the bottom, where lies the sensible world. If we take nothing with us to the top but our emptied, angelic intellects, we shall see nothing when we get there. Poe as God sits silent in darkness. Here the movement of tragedy is reversed: there is no action. Man as angel becomes a demon who cannot initiate the first motion of love, and we can feel only compassion with his suffering, for it is potentially ours."

I have argued earlier that Eliot has constantly and consciously addressed his poetry to the gentiles, and as a consequence has been forced to be not direct but indirect, since he could never assume agreement on principles or unanimity in doctrine. In the latter part of this lecture I may seem to have departed pretty far from such a thesis, but I think only apparently so. With regard to the apprehension of the eternal, all of us, even the professing Christians, are gentiles. We cannot see directly and face to face. We must use symbols and analogies. Eliot quite properly refuses to "overleap" and "cheat" the "condition of man." Man is not an angelic intelligence, a pure spirit. He is an embodied soul. Yet that body was created by God as was the world itself. God's purpose can be discerned in that world, and his glory can be shown forth through the creatures of that world. As the final chorus sings in *Murder in the Cathedral*:

> We praise Thee, O God, for Thy glory displayed in all the creatures of the earth,
> In the snow, in the rain, in the wind, in the storm; in all of Thy creatures, both the hunters and the hunted.
> For all things exist only as seen by Thee, only as known by Thee, all things exist
> Only in Thy light, and Thy glory is declared even in that which denies Thee; the darkness declares the glory of light.
> Those who deny Thee could not deny, if Thou didst not exist; and their denial is never complete, for if it were so, they would not exist.
> They affirm Thee in living; all things affirm Thee in living; the bird in the air, both the hawk and the finch; the beast on the earth, both the wolf and the lamb; the worm in the soil and the worm in the belly.
> Therefore man, whom Thou has made to be conscious of Thee, must consciously praise Thee, in thought and in word and in deed.

6.

R. P. WARREN

EXPERIENCE REDEEMED IN KNOWLEDGE

The poetry, the fiction, and even the critical essays of Robert Penn Warren form a highly unified and consistent body of work. But it would be impossible to reduce it, without distorting simplifications, to some thesis about human life. The work is not tailored to fit a thesis. In the best sense, it is inductive: it explores the human situation and tests against the fullness of human experience our various abstract statements about it. But Warren has his characteristic themes. He is constantly concerned with the meaning of the past and the need for one to accept the past if he is to live meaningfully in the present. In this concern there are resemblances to Faulkner, though Warren's treatment is his own. Again, there are resemblances to W. B. Yeats in Warren's almost obsessive concern to grasp the truth so that "all is redeemed / In knowledge." Again, as with Yeats, there is a tough-minded insistence upon the facts, including the realistic and ugly facts— a fierce refusal to shield one's eyes from what is there.

This commitment to the truth, and the deep sense that the truth is rarely simple, account for Warren's sharp scrutiny of the claims of rationality. He never glorifies irrationality: he is not the poet of the dark subliminal urges or the novelist with a mystique to exploit. But he does subject the claims of twentieth-century man to the sternest testing and he is suspicious of the doctrine of progress and of the blandishments of utopianism.

Faulkner's effective, though perhaps unwitting and unconscious, belief in original sin constitutes a bulwark against this heresy. Yeats' vigilant and unflagging resistance to what he calls "Whiggery" constitutes a similar safeguard. One could argue that, in general, the artist's commitment to the concrete situation and his need to focus upon the dramatic exigencies of the human predicament make it easier for him to reject this form of abstraction. Dedication to his art, then, would not necessarily bring the artist to Christianity. It would be foolish to claim *that*. But dedication to his art may well protect the artist from some of the deceptions endemic to our time. On the positive side, dedication to his art will probably help him at least to *see* the problems of the human spirit to which Christianity—and any other serious philosophy—addresses itself.

The work in which Robert Penn Warren challenges most directly some of the liberal secular ideas of our time is his long poem *Brother to Dragons*, published in 1953. It is about Thomas Jefferson, or rather about Jefferson's nephews, Lilburn and Isham Lewis, the sons of Jefferson's sister, Lucy Jefferson Lewis. The Lewises removed from Virginia to western Kentucky. There, after the death of their mother and after their father, Dr. Charles Lewis, had returned to Virginia, the two young men, Lilburn and Isham, murdered one of their slaves. On the night of December 15, 1811, the night when the New Madrid earthquake shook the Mississippi Valley, Lilburn, having called the other slaves together into the meathouse to witness what he was going to do, butchered on the meatblock a slave named George. George's offense had been to break a water pitcher on his way back from the spring to which he had been sent to fetch fresh water.

After some months, hints of the crime leaked out. Lilburn and Isham were indicted for murder, but before they could be arrested and put in jail, Lilburn was dead. Apparently the brothers had planned to stand, each on one side of their mother's grave, and shoot each other. When the sheriff's posse came up, Lilburn had been shot and was dying. Isham was captured, but while awaiting trial, broke jail and disappeared—to turn up, of all places, at the battle of New Orleans in 1815, one of the two Americans killed in that engagement. This, at least, was the story that the Kentucky riflemen brought back with them from New Orleans. In any case, the indictment naming Isham bears under the date March 20, 1815, the docket: "Ordered that this suit abate by the death of the defendant."

It is a fantastic story, a terrible and blood-chilling story. It is, however, a true story, with the documents on record. Thomas Jefferson must have been aware of the depths of wanton cruelty to which his nephews had sunk, but nowhere among the Jefferson Papers is there any reference to it. It is hard to imagine what the great Virginian who thought so much of man's possibilities, who penned the Declaration of Independence with its confident claims for man, who knew and was sympathetic to the French eighteenth-century rationalists—it is difficult and exciting to try to imagine what Jefferson's reaction must have been. This is the task that Warren takes upon himself. To my mind his effort of imaginative reconstruction results in a great and moving poem. That has been also the opinion of some of the most discerning critical minds here and in Great Britain. But not of all, I should add. For a great many Americans, Jefferson comes close to being a sacred figure, and to dare to portray a Jefferson troubled and in doubt, a Jefferson embittered and cynical, even though only temporarily, was to lay profane hands upon the idol. In fairness to Warren's conception of Jefferson, I should say that *Brother to Dragons* is not written in any spirit of debunking. It is a great Jefferson who emerges at the end of Warren's poem, a Jefferson who has, in giving up his more callow hopes in man, actually strengthened his basic belief in man's potentialities. At the end of the poem Jefferson is a chastened though not a disillusioned man.

A book-length poem does not adequately reveal itself in brief quotations. If I confine myself to quotations of reasonable length, I can hope to do no more than suggest something of the flavor of the poem. The impassioned dialectic and the stages of the drama through which the action works to its final resolution must be taken on faith unless one has read the poem. Yet I do want to quote two or three excerpts. Here is the way in which Warren imagines Jefferson's hopes for man as he sat down to write the Declaration of Independence:

> We knew we were only men
> Caught in our errors and interests. But I, a man,
> Suddenly saw in every face, face after face,
> The bleared, the puffed, the lank, the lean, all,
> On all saw the brightness blaze, and I knew my own days,
> Times, hopes, books, horsemanship, the praise of peers,
> Delight, desire, and even my love, but straw
> Fit for the flame, and in that fierce combustion I—
> Why, I was dead, I was nothing, nothing but joy,
> And my heart cried out, "Oh, this is Man!"
>
> And thus my minotaur. There at the blind
> Blank labyrinthine turn of my personal time,
> I met the beast. . . .
> . . . But no beast then: the towering
> Definition, angelic, arrogant, abstract,
> Greaved in glory, thewed with light, the bright
> Brow tall as dawn. I could not see the eyes.

So seized the pen, and in the upper room,
With the excited consciousness that I was somehow
Purged, rectified, and annealed, and my past annulled
And fate confirmed, wrote. And the bell struck
Far off in darkness, and the watch called out.
Time came, we signed the document, went home.
Slept, and I woke to the new self, and new doom.
I had not seen the eyes of that bright apparition.
I had been blind with light. That was my doom.
I did not know its eyes were blind.

I would like to quote also the poet's own commentary on man seen against the background of nature—man who is not "adjusted" to nature and can never be adjusted—who must live in an agony of will, and who finally in his need projects upon nature itself the struggle with circumstance that engages his own heart. The scene is winter, as it descends upon the Lewis brothers after their mother's death and burial:

And the year drove on. Winter. And from the Dakotas
The wind veers, gathers itself in ice-glitter
And star-gleam of dark, and finds the long sweep of the valley.
A thousand miles and the fabulous river is ice in the starlight.
The ice is a foot thick, and beneath, the water slides black like a dream,
And in the interior of that unpulsing blackness and thrilled zero
The big channel-cat sleeps with eye lidless, and the brute face
Is the face of the last torturer, and the white belly
Brushes the delicious and icy blackness of mud.
But there is no sensation. How can there be
Sensation when there is perfect adjustment? The blood
Of the creature is but the temperature of the sustaining flow:
The catfish is in the Mississippi and
The Mississippi is in the catfish and
Under the ice both are at one with God.
Would that we were!

By the end of the poem Jefferson can accept the past with its violence and evil; he is willing to acknowledge the fact of his kinship with his black-browed butcher of a nephew, and he exults that

> . . . nothing we had,
> Nothing we were,
> Is lost.
> All is redeemed,
> In knowledge.

Jefferson tells his sister that "without the fact of the past we cannot dream the future," and he remembers that he had once written to Adams, his old political rival and friend,

> To Adams, my old enemy and friend, that gnarled greatness, long ago.
> I wrote to him, and said
> That the dream of the future is better than the dream of the past.
> Now I should hope to find the courage to say
> That the dream of the future is not
> Better than the fact of the past, no matter how terrible.
> For without the fact of the past we cannot dream the future.

The necessity for accepting the past is the dominant theme of what is probably the best known of Warren's novels, *All the King's Men*. The task of making sense of history is the specific problem of its hero. Jack Burden is a young man who is trying to write his dissertation for a Ph.D. in history. His chosen topic is the life of an ancestor of his who died during the Civil War. The papers and documents have come down through the family to Jack. He has all the facts about this ancestor, Cass Mastern, but somehow the facts do not make sense to him. Cass Mastern as a young man was sent away to school at Transylvania College in Kentucky. While he was there he seduced—or perhaps it may be more accurate to say that he was seduced by—the wife of his friend, whose house he has frequently visited as a guest.

Later something occured to make Mastern realize that his friend's death by gunshot was not the accident that the world had supposed. His friend had somehow learned of the betrayal and had shot himself. Cass Mastern in his remorse tries in various ways to expiate his sin. When the Civil War breaks out, he refuses a commission, marches in the ranks, never firing a shot himself but courting the bullet that he hopes will find him. Finally, in 1864, the bullet does find him, and he dies in hospital of the infected wound. Jack Burden knows the facts, and even possesses Mastern's carefully kept and intimate journal, but he cannot understand why Mastern did what he did. This is the way in which Jack, speaking of himself in the third person, was able to put the matter some years later:

> I have said that Jack Burden could not put down the facts about Cass Mastern's world because he did not know Cass Mastern. Jack Burden did not say definitely to himself why he did not know Cass Mastern. But I (who am what Jack Burden became) look back now, years later, and try to say why.
>
> Cass Mastern lived for a few years and in that time he learned that the world is all of one piece. He learned that the world is like an enormous spider web and if you touch it, however lightly, at any point, the vibration ripples to the remotest perimeter and the drowsy spider feels the tingle and is drowsy no more but springs out to fling the gossamer coils about you who have touched the web and then inject the black, numbing poison under your hide. It does not matter whether or not you meant to brush the web of things. Your happy foot or your gay wing may have brushed it ever so lightly, but what happens always happens and there is the spider, bearded black and with his great faceted eyes glittering like mirrors in the sun, or like God's eye, and the fangs dripping.
>
> But how could Jack Burden, being what he was, understand that?

What Jack Burden was then, and how he later became something different constitute the matter of the novel. The knowledge that Jack's earlier life and his years at the university failed to give him, he learns painfully as a cynical newspaper reporter, watching, among other things, the meteoric career of Willie Stark as Stark rises to dictatorial power in this southern state. Through much of the course of the novel Jack Burden is acting as Stark's man Friday, advising him, doing various jobs for him, and, among these, applying his talents for historical research to the past lives of the governor's political opponents. What he is able to dig up usually disposes of that particular opponent. And, Jack cannot help noticing, there is usually something to dig up—no matter what the subject's reputation for probity. Once, when Jack demurs that there can be nothing to find in the past of the respectable Judge Irwin. Willie Stark assures Jack that there is always something: "Man is conceived in sin and born in corruption and he passeth from the stink of the didie to the stench of the shroud. There is always something."

There is not time, and for my purposes there is no need, to treat in detail the involved plot of this rich, violent, even melodramatic novel. Warren's novels are written with a kind of Elizabethan gusto. Though the school of criticism with which he is sometimes associated is charged with being overintellectual, formal, and even Alexandrian, Warren's own creative work, in its color and strident action, calls in question that oversimple account. Neither his poetry nor his fiction wear a prim and chilly formalism.

All the King's Men has been often described as a novel that depicts under a thin disguise the career of the late Huey P. Long. When the novel first appeared, a number of critics who should have known better disgraced themselves by their inability to make a distinction between the character of Willie Stark and that of the late senator from Louisiana. Certainly many things in the novel remind one of Louisiana under the Long regime; but this is a novel, not a biography, and finally—despite the importance of Willie Stark—the novel tells *Jack Burden's* story. The story of Willie Stark finally has its importance because of the way in which it affects the story of Jack. For as I said a few minutes ago, this novel is an account of how Jack Burden came to be a man capable of understanding the story of Cass Mastern—which means, of course, ultimately capable of understanding his own life and his relation to his parents, his friends, and the world.

Before Jack reaches this stage of knowledge, however, he has to be carried even further toward disillusionment and despair. For a time he comes to believe that man is a thing, a mere mechanism. He believes in what he calls "the Great Twitch." Men simply react to stimuli. Their actions are only more complicated versions of what happens when one runs an electric current through the severed legs of a frog. Given the stimulus, there is the automatic response.

The violence latent in the situation depicted in the novel finally comes to a head. Willie Stark is shot and killed by the young doctor Adam Stanton, who is Jack's boyhood friend; and Stanton himself is cut down by a fusillade fired by Stark's bodyguard. Moreover, Jack not only observes the death of his friends, he finds himself directly involved in violence, for he learns that he has been the unwitting cause of the death of his own father. For a time, as Jack tells us, his belief in the Great Twitch was a comfort, for if there was no God but the Great Twitch, then no man had any responsibility for anything, and he was somehow absolved from having caused his father's death. But later Jack tells us

> he woke up one morning to discover that he did not believe in the Great Twitch any more. He did not believe in it because he had seen too many people live and die. He had seen Lucy Stark and

> Sugar-Boy and the Scholarly Attorney and Sadie Burke and Anne Stanton live and the ways of their living had nothing to do with the Great Twitch. He had seen his father die. He had seen his friend Adam Stanton die. He had seen his friend Willie Stark die, and had heard him say with his last breath, "It might have been all different, Jack. You got to believe that."
>
> He had seen his two friends, Willie Stark and Adam Stanton, live and die. Each had killed the other. Each had been the doom of the other. As a student of history, Jack Burden could see that Adam Stanton, whom he came to call the man of idea, and Willie Stark, whom he came to call the man of fact, were doomed to destroy each other, just as each was doomed to try to use the other and to yearn toward and try to become the other, because each was incomplete with the terrible division of their age. But at the same time [that] Jack Burden came to see that his friends had been doomed, he saw that though doomed they had nothing to do with any doom under the godhead of the Great Twitch. They were doomed, but they lived in the agony of will.

The sobered and chastened Jack Burden, in his new knowledge and sympathy, is now actually able to understand and accept the man whom he had been brought up to believe was his father but whom from boyhood he had secretly despised because he felt that he lacked force and manhood. Now, long divorced from Jack's mother, the supposed father has become something of a religious fanatic—in the cynical young newspaperman's eyes, at least—writing religious tracts and doing good works in the slums of the city. But as the novel closes, Jack has brought him home to live out under Jack's protection the few months remaining to him. Jack even helps him with some of his tracts, since the old man, too feeble to write, can still dictate. One of the passages he dictates claims Jack's special attention:

> The creation of man whom God in His foreknowledge knew doomed to sin was the awful index of God's omnipotence. For it

would have been a thing of trifling and contemptible ease for Perfection to create mere perfection. To do so would, to speak truth, be not creation but extension. Separateness is identity and the only way for God to create, truly create, man was to make him separate from God Himself, and to be separate from God is to be sinful. The creation of evil is therefore the index of God's glory and His power. That had to *be* so that the creation of good might be the index of man's glory and power. But by God's help. By His help and in His wisdom."

He turned to me when he had spoken the last word, stared at me, and then said, "Did you put that down?"

"Yes," I replied.

Staring at me, he said with sudden violence, "It is true. I know it is true. Do you know it?"

I nodded my head and said yes. (I did so to keep his mind untroubled, but later I was not certain but that in my own way I did believe what he had said.)

The elder Mr. Burden's notion that man is "doomed to evil" veers toward the Manichaean heresy, but the truth that he is trying to render is evidently close to that to which Milton testified in *Paradise Lost*. Milton, of course, was careful to point out that man's fall was not *decreed* by God; yet God clearly did create the potentiality of evil as the necessary price to be paid for making man a free agent. Moreover, in His perfect foreknowledge, God knew that man would misuse his power to choose and that he would fall into sin. As God sums the doctrine up in Book III:

> I made [man] just and right,
> Sufficient to have stood, though free to fall.
> Such I created all th' Ethereal Powers
> And Spirits, both them who stood and them who faild;
> Freely they stood who stood, and fell who fell.
> Not free, what proof could they have givn sincere
> Of true allegiance, constant Faith or Love. . . .

Mr. Burden would evidently gloss the last three lines as follows: man *not* created free to fall would be merely an extension of God —no true creation.

Warren touches upon the problem of evil in a number of his poems. A very brilliant treatment is given in the momentarily bewildering poem entitled "Dragon Country." The country in question is, as the allusions in the poem make plain, Warren's native Kentucky. But as the dedication of the poem ("To Jacob Boehme") hints, the country in question is a country of the mind in which men encounter not human forces merely but principalities and powers. There is no reason, of course, why the two countries should not be one and the same, and in the poem they do coalesce. Indeed the brilliance of the poem comes in large part from the sense of the earthy and commonplace—"fence rails . . . splintered," "Mules torn from trace chains," the salesman traveling over the Kentucky hills "for Swift, or Armour"—and from the tone, colloquial, racy, and dry with a countryman's wit —both of which elements contrast with the preternatural horrors that are recounted, and thus give substance and solidity to them.

The reader of the poem may still ask "But why Kentucky?" And the answer would have to be: Kentucky, or any other Southern state. For the poem reflects the Southern experience, in which evil has an immediacy and reality that cannot be evaded or explained away. In that experience man is still confronted with the hard choice. He cannot simply call in the marriage counselor or the police or the psychiatrist. It is with this aspect of the Southern experience that "Dragon Country" deals.

We know, of course, that dragons simply do not exist. Yet what could have done the damage to Jack Simms' hogpen? And how account for some of the things that have happened since?

> So what, in God's name, could men think, when they couldn't
> bring to bay

> That belly-dragging earth-evil, but found that it took to air?
> Thirty-thirty or buckshot might fail, but then at least you could say
> You had faced it—assuming, of course, that you had survived the affair.
>
> We were promised troops, the Guard, but the Governor's skin got thin
> When up in New York the papers called him Saint George of Kentucky.
> Yes, even the Louisville reporters who came to Todd County would grin.
> Reporters, though rarely, still come. No one talks. They think it unlucky. . . .

Turned tongue-tied by the metropolitan press, not able to admit that the evil has reality, even the friends and relatives of the victims explain the facts away. When a man disappears, his family reports that he has gone to work in Akron, "or up to Ford, in Detroit." When Jebb Johnson's boot was found with a piece of his leg inside it, his mother refused to identify it as her son's.

Now land values are falling; lovers do not walk by moonlight. Certain fields are going back to brush and undergrowth. The coon "dips his little black paw" undisturbed each night in the stream.

> Yes, other sections have problems somewhat different from ours.
> Their crops may fail, bank rates rise, on rumor of war loans be called,
> But we feel removed from maneuvers of Russia, or other great powers,
> And from much ordinary hope are now disenthralled.
>
> The Catholics have sent in a mission, Baptists report new attendance.
> But that's not the point. We are human, and the human heart
> Demands language for reality that has no slightest dependence
> On desire, or need. Now in church they pray only that evil depart.

But if the Beast were withdrawn now, life might dwindle again
To the ennui, the pleasure, and night sweat, known in the time
before
Necessity of truth had trodden the land, and heart, to pain,
And left, in darkness, the fearful glimmer of joy, like a spoor.

But this last difficult stanza is no Manichaean celebration of evil. The poem is not simply saying how much better off are the Kentuckians who inhabit the dragon's country, because they have to live so dangerously. The "fearful glimmer of joy" that the last line hints of comes not from evil as such but from the "necessity of truth." Admitting the element of horror in life, conceding the element of mystery, facing the terrifying truth—these are the only actions that can promise the glimmer of ultimate joy.

It is almost a misnomer to say that Warren's poem "Original Sin" is about the problem of evil at all. In the context of this poem "evil" is too specific a term, but, as we shall see, the poem does deal with a related problem.

ORIGINAL SIN: A SHORT STORY

Nodding, its great head rattling like a gourd,
And locks like seaweed strung on the stinking stone,
The nightmare stumbles past, and you have heard
It fumble your door before it whimpers and is gone:
It acts like the old hound that used to snuffle your door and moan.

You thought you had lost it when you left Omaha,
For it seemed connected then with your grandpa, who
Had a wen on his forehead and sat on the veranda
To finger the precious protuberance, as was his habit to do,
Which glinted in sun like rough garnet or the rich old brain
bulging through.

But you met it in Harvard Yard as the historic steeple
Was confirming the midnight with its hideous racket,

And you wondered how it had come, for it stood so imbecile,
With empty hands, humble, and surely nothing in pocket:
Riding the rods, perhaps—or grandpa's will paid the ticket.

You were almost kindly then, in your first homesickness,
As it tortured its stiff face to speak, but scarcely mewed;
Since then you have outlived all your homesickness,
But have met it in many another distempered latitude:
Oh, nothing is lost, ever lost! at last you understood.

But it never came in the quantum glare of sun
To shame you before your friends, and had nothing to do
With your public experience or private reformation:
But it thought no bed too narrow—it stood with lips askew
And shook its great head sadly like the abstract Jew.

Never met you in the lyric arsenical meadows
When children call and your heart goes stone in the bosom;
At the orchard anguish never, nor ovoid horror,
Which is furred like a peach or avid like the delicious plum.
It takes no part in your classic prudence or fondled axiom.

Not there when you exclaimed: "Hope is betrayed by
Disastrous glory of sea-capes, sun-torment of whitecaps
—There must be a new innocence for us to be stayed by."
But there it stood, after all the timetables, all the maps,
In the crepuscular clutter of *always*, *always*, or *perhaps*.

You have moved often and rarely left an address,
And hear of the deaths of friends with a sly pleasure,
A sense of cleansing and hope, which blooms from distress;
But it has not died, it comes, its hand childish, unsure,
Clutching the bribe of chocolate or a toy you used to treasure.

It tries the lock; you hear, but simply drowse:
There is nothing remarkable in that sound at the door.
Later you may hear it wander the dark house
Like a mother who rises at night to seek a childhood picture;

> Or it goes to the backyard and stands like an old horse cold in the
> pasture.

The subtitle is "A short story." The poem is a kind of narrative, the account of a man haunted by a nightmare. The words "Original Sin" may be thought to tell us what the nightmare is, and they certainly give a clue, but they can be a distraction if we take our conception of original sin too rigidly from either Aquinas or Calvin, or even tailor it to meet the requirements of Sigmund Freud. The meaning of the nightmare rests upon a reading of the poem itself.

There is another clue worth mentioning at the outset: like many another Warren poem, in "Original Sin" the protagonist is referred to quite casually as "you." The implication is that the nightmare belongs to everyman. The nightmare's great head is an empty head: it rattles "like a gourd." But its nodding, it becomes plain, is not a gesture of intelligence—a sign of recognition or assent—it is merely the bobbing, the awkwardly carried, too-heavy head; for the nightmare is as witless as a hydrocephalic child. It cannot form words; it whimpers or mews: its hand is childish and unsure as it clutches the bribe of chocolate or the "toy you used to treasure."

In the poem the nightmare is associated with childhood; you had thought of it as being a part of your childhood world, a world that included grandpa with the curious wen on his head, sitting on the veranda in Omaha. It shocked you, therefore, when the nightmare turned up, of all places, in Harvard Yard, but after the first shock, you in your first homesickness were almost glad to see it. Hideous though it was, you felt almost kindly toward it. But whether you feel kindly toward it or loathe it, you cannot shake it off. This is presumably what "at last you understood": that nothing is ever lost—that the past can never be escaped. If the poem ended here, we might be tempted to think that the nightmare stood merely for the past—the monstrous and irrational world of the child's nightmare. But the poem does not end here. The stanzas that follow show that the nightmare is much more than the ghost of the past.

Those stanzas describe the occasion on which the nightmare appears and the kind of occasion in which it remains decently absent. For imbecilic though it is, the nightmare observes what amounts to a gentlemanly code. It forbears to shame you before your friends. It also remains hidden at the moments of apparent intellectual vision and at moments of emotional crisis. It has nothing to do with the experience of poignant beauty—the "lyric arsenical meadows when children call," nor with the pang of Gethsemane agony—the "orchard anguish," nor with the moment of terror, when horror has come to fruition and hangs like a ripened fruit, asking to be tasted, to be gorged.

The nightmare also absents itself from those occasions of calculation in which you fondle the axioms by which you live. It was absent, for example, when you made the brave resolution to begin over again and to found yourself upon a "new innocence." At that moment of insight it became clear to you that what betrays us is the multiplicity of experience. Therefore we must resolve not to allow ourselves to be distracted by that multiplicity, even though it may seem at times rich and glorious. We must demand better charts: we must strictly adhere to the charts, and thus keep ourselves from being swallowed up in the welter of our multiform world. Yet, after all the "time tables, all the maps," there you suddenly saw the nightmare, standing in the twilight clutter of "*always, always, or perhaps.*"

This crepuscular clutter may at first seem a different sort from that of the "sun-torment of whitecaps" by which the speaker says that "Hope is betrayed." Yet both are multiplicity, even though one is sunlit and the other twilit. The best predictions somehow go awry; calculation miscalculates. The confidently voiced proposition has to be revised downward from an assertion of truth to a claim for probability—the confident *always* gives way to the lame *perhaps*.

The nightmare is much more than the ghost of the past: it is associated with the contingent element in the universe, that factor which renders the best timetables inaccurate, the most carefully surveyed maps, defective. In a world which aspires to a certain neat precision, contingency is indeed a nightmare, subhuman in its lack of conscious purpose, slovenly with its unkempt locks "like seaweed strung on the stinking stone." For the nightmare inhabits a world which defies the logical ordering of our daylight, working world. Since it is irrational, it is therefore monstrous: the timetable can find no place for it.

As we have seen, the nightmare avoids the glare of full day and the glare of full consciousness. Most often it comes to you in the twilight fringe of consciousness. Half asleep, you hear it fumble at the lock. You sense that it is in the house. Later, you may hear it wander from room to room. It moves about "Like a mother who rises at night to seek a childhood picture" or it stands outside "like an old horse cold in the pasture." To what do these comparisons point? They occur in the climactic position in the poem; they are surely more than casual analogies.

If we look back through the poem, we find that "it" has been compared to a child, to an imbecile, to an animal (though a faithful domestic animal like the old hound or the old horse), and now, to the mother. All of these are types of subrationality or irrationality, for even the mother acts in disregard of—or in excess of—the claims of rationality. The picture will keep until daylight; it will be the easier found by daylight. But, obsessed with her need, she rises at night to fumble patiently through the darkened rooms. It is a childhood picture. The child has presumably left the house—has perhaps long since become a man, and put away childish things. But the mother yearns toward the child that was. There is no use in reasoning with her, for her claim transcends reason; and, anyway, she will be happier left to her search.

But the things to which the nightmare is compared have something else in common; none of them has anything to do with the realm of practical affairs. The child and the idiot obviously do not have, but neither does the mother, the hound, or the horse. They are all superannuated: the old hound snuffling at the door, and the old horse turned out to pasture, and the mother living in the past. The reference to the timetables and the maps is relevant after all, for maps and timetables are the instruments of action, abstract descriptions of our world in which the world is stripped down to be acted upon; and all action has a future reference. Yet the future grows out of the past, and is, we may say if we think in terms of pure efficiency, always contaminated by the past. Our experiments never work out perfectly because we can never control all the conditions: we never have chemically pure ingredients, a perfectly clean test tube, absolutely measured quantities. Most of all, we ourselves are not clean test tubes.

Indeed, as the next-to-the-last stanza makes clear, the nightmare is the irrational being who lies at the depths of your own being, for it comes "Clutching a toy you used to treasure." It is the you that cannot be disowned, even though as you grow older you hear "of the deaths of friends with a sly pleasure," feeling in spite of yourself "A sense of cleansing and hope," knowing that one more tie with the past and with that irrational you has been broken.

The new innocence, for which the speaker, bewildered by the sun-torment of whitecaps, cries out, would be aseptic, chemically pure; but we ourselves are never that. Animal man, instinctive man, passionate man—these represent deeper layers of our nature than does rational man. Considered from the standpoint of pure rationality, these subrational layers are, as we have seen, a contamination, something animal—or actually worse than animal, imbecilic, an affront to our pride in reason. But it is in these subrational layers that our highest values, loyalty, patience, sympathy, love are ultimately rooted. These virtues are not the constructions of pure rationality, and so the comparisons with which the poem ends—to the mother, yearning past reason for the childhood picture, and to the old horse, patient in the cold pasture—are once more relevant.

I have interpreted the poem as a critique of secularizing rationality, and by doing so have risked oversimplifying it. We must not simplify the poem into a tract or a sermon. It is a poem, which means that it has its own drama. Its meaning cannot, without essential loss, be detached from the drama. Dramatic tension is maintained throughout the poem: the revulsion of horror, the necessary association of the horror with the past, and specifically with one's own past; the false confidence that one has escaped it; the sick realization that one cannot escape it—these are dynamically related to each other. Not least important, one should add, is the speaker's final attitude as the poem closes: I should not describe it as mere passive acceptance; it is certainly more than cynical bitterness. It may even contain a wry kind of ironic comfort: the listener drowses off in the consciousness that, moving about or merely patiently waiting, "it" is there, and can be counted upon to remain.

But any paraphrase blurs the richness and complexity of the final attitude. The poet is not telling us *about* the experience; he is *giving* us the experience. For the full meaning the reader has to be referred to the poem itself. The poem is hard to summarize, not because of its vagueness but because of its precision. "What it says"—the total experience, which includes the speaker's attitude as a part of it—the total experience can be conveyed by no document less precise than the poem itself. The full experience —the coming to terms with reality, or with God, or with one's deepest self, cannot be stated directly, for it is never an abstract description. It can be given to us only dramatically, which means indirectly.

In a sense, then, the poem constitutes a kind of concrete instance of our problem as well as a statement of it. This poem—and any poem, I should say—makes use of a method of indirection. The truth of a poem does not reside in a formula. It cannot be got at by mere logic. Poetry itself is incommensurable with charts and timetables. It is a piece of—perhaps I should say an "imitation" of—our fluid and multiform world. That is why fewer and fewer people can read such poems as this. Perhaps if we could read poetry, we might understand our plight better: not merely because we could hear what our poets have to tell us about our world but because the very fact that we could read the poems would itself testify to an enlargement of our powers of apprehension—would testify to a transcendence of a world abstracted to formula and chart. A growing inability to read poetry may conversely point to a narrowing of apprehension, to a hardening of the intellectual arteries which will leave us blind to all but that world of inflexible processes and arid formulas which may be our doom.

Warren's characteristic theme—man's obligation to find the truth by which he lives—comes in for a fine restatement in a recent poem and a recent novel. Both put a young soldier's idealism to the test; both have a Civil War setting. The poem is entitled "Harvard '61: Battle Fatigue." The young Harvard man of the class of 1861 has died in the fight to free the slaves, but in death he is puzzled—even nettled—by the fact that others have died bravely for a bad cause—or perhaps, for no cause at all.

> I didn't mind dying—it wasn't that at all.
> It behooves a man to prove manhood by dying for Right.
> If you die for Right that fact is your dearest requital,

> But you find it disturbing when others die who simply haven't
> the right.

The way in which certain "unprincipled wastrels of blood and profligates of breath" have flung themselves into death has confused the issues. There was, for example, the middle-aged Confederate soldier whom he shot and killed just before he received his own death wound. The man was, he exclaimed to himself, "old as my father" and the dying Confederate soldier, observing the boy's blanched face, had even given him a bit of fatherly advice, saying to him: "Buck up! If it hadn't been you, / Some other young squirt would a-done it."

But even as the young Harvard idealist heard these words,

> The tumult of battle went soundless, like gesture in dream. And
> I was dead, too.
>
> Dead, and had died for the Right, as I had a right to,
> And glad to be dead, and hold my residence
> Beyond life's awful illogic, and the world's stew,
> Where people who haven't the right just die, with ghastly
> impertinence.

The young idealist has a case: he had indeed tried to slay "without rancor" and had striven to keep his heart pure "though hand took stain." In a sense, then, he has earned a certain right to his squeamishness. In any case, such squeamishness touches some answering chord in the hearts of all of us nowadays who regard war as the ultimate horror and justify, if at all, our participation in it only in terms of its necessity and our own purity of purpose. As for the poet's attitude toward the idealistic young fighter for the right, "Harvard '61" is only one half of a double poem, the other member of which has to do with the gnarled and bewhiskered Confederate whom the young man killed. The inclusive title for this double poem is, significantly, "Two Studies in Idealism: Short Survey of American, and Human, History." The poet is not condemning idealism but extending our conventional notions of it and in the process showing how deeply it is rooted in human nature. If the member of the class of '61 is being chided, it is not for his dedication or his bravery but for a too-simple view of reality and a certain pharisaical self-righteousness.

In his latest novel, *Wilderness*, Warren addresses himself once more to the problem of the idealist caught up in the Civil War. His criticism of idealism has not changed, but in this instance his treatment of the idealist is not glancing and ironic but direct, serious, and fully and obviously sympathetic.

The hero of the novel is a young Bavarian Jew, Adam Rosenzweig. He has a club foot, but in spite of this deformity and in spite of the bitter opposition of his uncle—his only close relative, for Adam's parents are dead—he makes his way to America in order to take part in the War to help free the slaves.

What Adam finds, of course, is the mixture of good and evil, the contradictions and cross purposes, that one always encounters in a great war. He finds, for example, that the inhabitants of New York City are not unanimous in regarding the conflict as a holy war for freedom. Some of them even resent the Negroes as being the indirect cause of their being conscripted to fight. Adam finds himself caught up in such a conscription riot on the very day that he lands. The mob is killing such Negroes as it can find.

The general situation in which Adam finds himself has an aspect more troubling still. As he makes his way toward the battlefields, his immediate companions turn out to be men who are vicious or cowardly or callous. Though he is sorry for the Negro Mose Talbutt and tries to teach him to read, he finds it hard to accept him fully or even to come to a genuine liking of him. Though he applauds Jed Hawksworth for having displayed the sense of justice and integrity that forced him to leave his native South, Adam cannot find in Hawksworth a brother idealist or even a warm human being. In sum, Adam's persistent difficulty is that of accepting man with all of his imperfections and believing that the ideal can have any place in a creature so faulty.

In the stinking mud of the army's winter quarters in northern Virginia, the sensitive young man is almost overwhelmed with the ugliness and cruelty and crassness of human life. A soldier celebrated for heroic exploits in battle turns out to be in the camp a drunken bully. An ignorant washerwoman who hangs around the camp is sentenced to the lash for prostitution and Adam hears her shrieks as the whip falls. The state of affairs seems to call in question everything that he has lived for up to this time and the whole meaning of his quest.

The last two chapters of this short novel bring to a head this crisis in Adam's affairs. He has slipped away from the wagon train and driven his sutler's vehicle into the Wilderness where the confused and bloody battle will be fought. He is at last alone. The battle will eventually reach into the glade where his team is tethered. There he will face an ultimate testing of his conception of human kind and of reality.

Few authors would have dared to compress so many successive states of mind into so short a time span, as Adam's mood shifts from dejected loneliness to tender affection, or from obsessive guilt to pride in his new-found masculine power, or from cynicism to human sympathy, before he finally attains to self-knowledge and through that knowledge to a way of accepting humankind. Certainly few authors could have brought it off. But Warren has earlier set forth very skillfully the circumstances which have made Adam what he is and the psychological pattern through which Adam will be forced to move. Moreover, the battlefield itself so eagerly sought by Adam, and won to with such difficulty, provides the necessary forcing bed for Adam's development. There he finds himself detached from and yet a part of the battle, in the "cold center of stillness in the storm which was the world." There is opportunity for thought, yet involvement is imminent. Finally, after the skirmishers strike into his hidden glade, fight over Adam's almost passive body, and then rush away, the burning forest, which has been set afire by the guns, forces Adam toward decision and action.

But unless the reader already possesses the supporting context, including Adam's earlier history, there is little point in trying here to lead him step by step through the drama of Adam's development. No summary, in any case, can preserve the drama. But it will do no harm to mention some of the elements at work in Adam's Wilderness experience.

The day begins with a pang of loneliness as Adam wakes from a dream of his mother, the mother who, he feels, had at the end come to hate him because he sided with his father in believing that it was right to sacrifice one's family in the fight for liberty. Though his mother had not forgiven him, he yearns for forgiveness. In the dream she had seemed to proffer tenderness and love.

There is Adam's sense of guilt. In particular, he feels remorse for the exasperation which allowed him to lash out at Mose Crawford, the freedman, the night before Mose murdered his tormentor, Jed Hawksworth. Adam believes that his bitter words may have actually triggered the deed. In the silence of the forest, Adam wonders about something else: why did not Mose kill *him*, the man who had actually uttered the harsh words, rather than Jed, and he reflects that the reason must be that Mose had once saved his life: "he thought, *you cannot strike down what you have lifted up*. So Jed, he decided, had had to die in his place." In a curious way, Jed's life has been sacrificed for his own, and he wonders whether "every man is, in the end, a sacrifice for every other man."

Adam's reveries are interrupted when the battle bursts in upon him. A handful of ragged Confederate soldiers overrun the glade, knock Adam down, and, while one of them, a mere boy, sits on Adam's almost passive body, these half-starved men stuff themselves from the supplies in Adam's sutler's wagon. But their hunger humanizes them for Adam: he "felt a sweet sadness fill his heart. He loved the boy because the boy had been very hungry and now had food." The psychology here is sound enough: it is always easier for the Adams of our world to accept the fact that they share a basic humanity with the enemy than to accept the evident bestiality within their allies or the latent bestiality within themselves. For Adam, that more difficult acceptance is late in coming.

First, a detachment of Federal troops surprises the Confederates; then in the ensuing fight Adam manages to reach a rifle and kills one of the Confederate soldiers. The Federal troops rush away in pursuit of the enemy, and Adam once more finds himself alone. He experiences a moment of pride in the proof that, though crippled, he is man enough to act and kill. But his momentary pride flickers out into dejection and bitterness. He is lost in the forest and barefoot—one of the retreating Confederates has taken Adam's boots, including the one carefully fashioned by a Bavarian cobbler especially for his deformed foot. Adam has lost his team: one horse has been killed; the other has run away. He finds himself again questioning his motives for having come to America. Perhaps he had come simply to justify himself. He weighs too the consequences of this coming: besides being responsible for the death of the Confederate soldier, is he not responsible also for the death of Jed Hawskworth?

In his bitterness he feels that the world has betrayed him—even his father, who bequeathed him the idealism that forced him toward the conflict for freedom but who also bequeathed the deformed foot that renders him unable to become freedom's soldier—even his father has betrayed him. For a moment he decides to accept the betrayal. Henceforth he will be tough-minded and hard-boiled. As he walks over to strip the boots from the dead soldier, he feels that he has at last discovered the nature of the world. All that he had previously believed was false. The bitter discovery actually gives him a sense of release and of power. Now at last he knows the truth about reality.

Hardened by this new and devastating knowledge, he tells himself, as he stares at the face of the soldier whom he has killed: "I killed him because his foot was not like mine." This remark is, of course, a fantastic oversimplification, but it does at least testify to Adam's having peered into the depths of himself and having glimpsed the dark side of his own motivation: specifically, the fact that his crippled foot has indeed had its part in his desire to engage in this war. But as he tries to put on the dead soldier's boots, his glance happens to fall upon the phylactery and the talith which he has brought from Bavaria and which, though he had given up his religion, he had never been quite able to bring himself to throw away. In the looting of the wagon, they have been tossed aside. Seeing them, he is suddenly smitten with a sense of desolation. He takes off the dead man's boots and sets them down tidily near the corpse. "In a numb, quiet way he thought how foolish this was." And yet he has to do it. He peers again into the dead man's face and tries to see whether it shows any mark of the young man's life. He wonders how his own dead face will look and asks himself the question: "Am I different from other men?"

The redness in the sky tells him that the forest is now on fire, set aflame by the guns, and he realizes that he ought to go and drag the wounded away from the flames. He strains his ears to hear the cries of the wounded, but he can hear only the imagined cries within his own head. Suddenly, he finds himself praying the prayers that he had learned as a boy: "Have mercy upon the remnant of the flock of Thy hand, and say unto the Destroying Angel, Stay thy hand."

As the book ends, Adam is ready to rise and try to make his rescue. In a sense it will be what he has to do, just as his coming across the sea and joining in the fight for freedom was what he has had to do. But he has broken "the compulsion of the dream" which has held him up to this time. It is not that his action in seeking to fight for freedom, because it was a compulsive action, has been wrong. He knows that he would do it again, but now he cries "in his inwardness: *But, oh, with a different heart!*" He prepares to pick up the dead man's boots (with a different heart he can now accept them), put them on, and hobble out of the forest glade.

What has happened, of course, is that Adam has discovered himself and, now understanding himself, can forgive, and ask forgiveness of, his parents; can accept the past; and can enter into communion with mankind. His experience parallels in general terms the experience of several of Warren's other characters—it is like that of Jack Burden at the end of *All the King's Men*, or that of the heroine of *Band of Angels*, who hates her father for what he has done to her and only at the end finds herself able to forgive him, to accept her past, and thus to find freedom.

This matter of man's relation to the ideal runs through the fiction and the poetry of Warren. A Christian may be tempted to transpose the problem into that of conversion or redemption. But if he yields to the temptation, he must take the responsibility for the transposition and not assume that it formed part of the author's intention. Still, there is no doubt that one can learn from Warren's fiction and poetry a great deal about the psychology of conversion and the cost of redemption even though Warren himself poses his problems in non-Christian terms—often in terms of the movement from ignorance to knowledge or from bafflement and confusion to order and insight.

Warren's poem "Walk by Moonlight in a Small Town" is a beautiful instance. The speaker returns to his boyhood home and finds the little town, in spite of all its tawdry "matter of fact," filled to the brim with mystery.

> And pitiful was the moon-bare ground.
> Dead grass, the gravel, earth ruined and raw—
> It had not changed. And then I saw
> That children were playing, with no sound.
> They ceased their play, then quiet as moonlight,
> drew, slow, around.
>
> Their eyes were fixed on me, and I
> Now tried, face by pale face, to find
> The names that haunted in my mind.
> Each small, upgazing face would lie
> Sweet as a puddle, and silver-calm, to the night sky.
>
> But something grew in their pale stare:
> Nor reprobation or surprise,
> Nor even forgiveness in their eyes,
> But a humble question dawning there,
> From face to face, like beseechment dawning on empty air.

Here the children remembered from his boyhood put the question to him, not he to them. It is a question that he would answer, but obviously no man can answer.

> Might a man but know his Truth, and might
> He live so that life, by moon or sun,
> In dusk or dawn, would be all one,
> Then never on a summer night
> Need he stand and shake in that cold blaze of Platonic light.

But what the poet says here is humanly impossible. Man can never know his truth so thoroughly that he will not need to shake in the cold blaze of the light of the ideal. It is a beautiful poem and the Christian may perhaps be forgiven for boldly appropriating it as a tender though completely unsentimental statement of the way in which the whole human creation yearns toward the truth that would give it significance and thus redeem it from its all-too-evident mutability into eternity. But how honest the poem is! For the desiderated truth is a judgment as well as a revelation.

A CONCLUDING NOTE

In the course of these lectures I have been able to deal with only five authors. A larger selection from twentieth-century writers who are of significance to the Christian reader, and to any serious reader, would make my general case much more impressive. Yet even these five examples may be sufficient to indicate why one can say that our modern literature is not only brilliant in its own right but a literature which ought to fill a thoughtful Christian with a sense of real exhilaration. To be frank, it is a literature which is very much finer than we deserve. It is literature with which many of us who profess to be Christians have had less than nothing to do, since many of us who are Christians are not even aware that it exists, or since many who are aware of it continue to dismiss it as merely sensational, violent, meaningless, or nihilistic.

It is not a recording of meaningless violence. Taken at the lowest discount, these writers—to revert to Tillich's point once more—make an affirmation of the manhood of man and dramatize his resistance to the tendencies of our culture that would turn him into a mere thing. This resistance is a central theme in much of Hemingway's fiction—witness his stories about courage and about man's gallant if desperate attempts to create a tiny bit of order and decency within a disordered universe. Like Hemingway, Faulkner emphasizes courage and the need to cleave to some ideal of honor which will redeem man from mere bestiality or mere mechanism. But with Faulkner, of course, we are dealing with a writer who comes out of a traditional society, a society that has a religious substructure, and the Christian component of which, in spite of perversions and distortions, is very much alive. These distortions—especially since they are not dead but full of vitality—account for Faulkner's anti-Calvinism and anti-clericalism, but Faulkner's work itself incorporates a great deal of residual Christianity. Faulkner's is, to be sure, a Christianity which is tilted over toward man's need for vindication as man, and one which stresses man's ability to endure any hardship in order to secure that vindication, but it also includes instances of self-sacrifice and expiation, of pity and love.

Yet as earlier pages have made plain, Faulkner's is a very mixed case. His fiction raises a general problem of considerable importance in the literature of our time. At the risk of great over-simplification, one can put it in this way: with the breakup of the Christian synthesis, nature and history have tended to fall apart, and the poet or novelist today often is to be found preoccupied with one or the other, or with first one, then the other—in some extreme cases even having come to worship one or the other. Can the modern writer bring history and nature into a meaningful relation that does not absorb one into the other?

The believers in progress and the Utopians generally are concerned with history. Man is now arriving (or will soon arrive) at a mastery of history. When he attains this mastery, he will direct and control his destiny. History as man will make it in the future can be counted on to improve upon nature and remove its deficiencies. If the writer is sufficiently an activist (like some of the Marxist writers of the 1930s) he may move out of literature altogether, frankly conceiving his task as that of propagandist for a program. But many a writer who is less extreme in his cultishness and who rejects the Marxist interpretation of history will still count it of primary importance that he shall deal with matters of the proper historical relevance. The game is to pick out which is really the mounting wave of the future and then to ride it triumphantly onto the beach. The really disabling failure is to dither about in some backwater.

Other writers, however, tend to exalt nature. They are impressed with the difficulty that man has had in his efforts to master nature, and with the fact that despite all its changes, nature does not essentially change, but through the round of the seasons and of the centuries, and even through all the cycles of civilization's growth and decay, shows a changeless immortality. The poetry of William Butler Yeats, with his cyclic theory of history, would yield examples. But the celebration of nature is not tied to a cyclic theory of history. Even purer instances of such celebration would be found in the poetry of Dylan Thomas or in that of Wallace Stevens, who descants tirelessly and often very beautifully on the endlessly shifting world about us, which is an incitement to man's imagination, which provides the imagination with the pigments by which, and the canvas upon which, it paints its vision, and yet which constitutes the very ground in which man and his imagination are rooted. It is interesting to notice, by the way, how much very brilliant nature poetry our modern writers have produced. One thinks of Hemingway, for example, and of Yeats and Faulkner and Warren as well. Faulkner's *Go Down, Moses* and *The Hamlet* contain what can be described adequately only as great hymns to nature.

It is significant, however, that most of the writers discussed in these five lectures are still trying to relate history and nature. Warren is very much interested in history. History is a dominant theme in much of the later poetry of Yeats. History is almost an obsession for the characters of Faulkner's great novels. History reveals itself as the powerful undertheme of Eliot's *Four Quartets*.

Perhaps it is a mark of the wholeness of these writers that all of them are trying in their various ways to make some kind of synthesis of history and nature. For them, man does, and does not, dominate the world. Theirs is a world in which, despite its beauty and despite man's creatureliness, man is in some way an alien. If a part of nature, he is also in some sense now cut off from nature, and cannot hope to re-establish an easy rapport with nature. On the other hand, though man must strive with nature and in some sense against nature, he cannot hope to dominate nature, and must learn to fear it, respect it, and finally love it.

The way in which our five writers are aware of this nature-history tension and reflect it in their work—even in Yeats, it is clearly evident—testifies to the continuing importance of a substratum of Christianity. Be that as it may, the way in which this nature-history tension shows in these writers is of very great importance to us—so important that even when it seems to be simply another symptom of our disordered civilization, it constitutes a further recommendation of their work. For we read literary works not so much for instruction in ideas as to learn—through a kind of dramatic presentation—what it feels like to hold certain beliefs, including the pressures exerted against belief. The finest artists of our time, even those who are avowed Christians, will, as a matter of necessity, reflect in their work some of the difficulties of belief. So it is, as we have seen, with the poetry of T. S. Eliot; and his awareness of the pressure of a secular culture renders his poetry more valuable to us rather than less valuable.

The value of any poet or novelist is in direct proportion to this honesty of reporting and totality of perception, for these are the fundamental virtues of all literary art and give the writer his primary role in the human economy. That role is to give us an awareness of our world, not as an object viewed in clinical detachment, not as mere mechanism, but of our world as it involves ourselves—in part a projection of ourselves, in part an impingement upon ourselves. In making us see our world for what it is, the artist also makes us see ourselves for what we are. As Coleridge long ago observed, the poet's task is to awake the mind's attention "from the lethargy of custom," to remove "the film of familiarity" that obscures the world before us, and to give us a renewed vision of reality.

Where there is no vision the people perish. When such imaginative vision is not constantly renewed, the very faculty of imagination atrophies. A decisive aspect of man's dehumanization—perhaps the critical point in his transition from man into thing—occurs when he loses his power to comprehend his world except in terms of mechanical adjustments to the narrower exigencies of materialistic life. The death of the imagination is thus a stage in the death of the spirit. The crowd that the protagonist of *The Waste Land* saw through "the brown fog of a winter dawn" flowing across London Bridge had suffered death in just this sense:

> A crowd flowed over London Bridge, so many,
> I had not thought death had undone so many.
> Sighs, short and infrequent, were exhaled,
> And each man fixed his eyes upon his feet.

If one of the functions of literature is to help us to fix our eyes otherwhere, another important function and perhaps a primary function is to let us see where we actually do fix our eyes—to reveal the predicament in which we gaze idly at nothing except that which is just beyond our noses and merely beneath our feet.

INDEX

THE YALE PAPERBOUNDS

Y-1 LIBERAL EDUCATION AND THE DEMOCRATIC IDEAL *by A. Whitney Griswold*
Y-2 A TOUCH OF THE POET *by Eugene O'Neill*
Y-3 THE FOLKLORE OF CAPITALISM *by Thurman Arnold*
Y-4 THE LOWER DEPTHS AND OTHER PLAYS *by Maxim Gorky*
Y-5 THE HEAVENLY CITY OF THE EIGHTEENTH-CENTURY PHILOSOPHERS *by Carl Becker*
Y-6 LORCA *by Roy Campbell*
Y-7 THE AMERICAN MIND *by Henry Steele Commager*
Y-8 GOD AND PHILOSOPHY *by Etienne Gilson*
Y-9 SARTRE *by Iris Murdoch*
Y-10 AN INTRODUCTION TO THE PHILOSOPHY OF LAW *by Roscoe Pound*
Y-11 THE COURAGE TO BE *by Paul Tillich*
Y-12 PSYCHOANALYSIS AND RELIGION *by Erich Fromm*
Y-13 BONE THOUGHTS *by George Starbuck*
Y-14 PSYCHOLOGY AND RELIGION *by C. G. Jung*
Y-15 EDUCATION AT THE CROSSROADS *by Jacques Maritain*
Y-16 LEGENDS OF HAWAII *by Padraic Colum*
Y-17 AN INTRODUCTION TO LINGUISTIC SCIENCE *by E. H. Sturtevant*
Y-18 A COMMON FAITH *by John Dewey*
Y-19 ETHICS AND LANGUAGE *by Charles L. Stevenson*
Y-20 BECOMING *by Gordon W. Allport*
Y-21 THE NATURE OF THE JUDICIAL PROCESS *by Benjamin N. Cardozo*
Y-22 PASSIVE RESISTANCE IN SOUTH AFRICA *by Leo Kuper*
Y-23 THE MEANING OF EVOLUTION *by George Gaylord Simpson*
Y-24 PINCKNEY'S TREATY *by Samuel Flagg Bemis*
Y-25 TRAGIC THEMES IN WESTERN LITERATURE *edited by Cleanth Brooks*
Y-26 THREE STUDIES IN MODERN FRENCH LITERATURE *by J. M. Cocking, Enid Starkie, and Martin Jarrett-Kerr*
Y-27 WAY TO WISDOM *by Karl Jaspers*
Y-28 DAILY LIFE IN ANCIENT ROME *by Jérôme Carcopino*
Y-29 THE CHRISTIAN IDEA OF EDUCATION *edited by Edmund Fuller*
Y-30 FRIAR FELIX AT LARGE *by H. F. M. Prescott*
Y-31 THE COURT AND THE CASTLE *by Rebecca West*
Y-32 SCIENCE AND COMMON SENSE *by James B. Conant*
Y-33 THE MYTH OF THE STATE *by Ernst Cassirer*

Y–34 Frustration and Aggression *by John Dollard et al.*
Y–35 The Integrative Action of the Nervous System *by Sir Charles Sherrington*
Y–36 Toward a Mature Faith *by Erwin R. Goodenough*
Y–37 Nathaniel Hawthorne *by Randall Stewart*
Y–38 Poems *by Alan Dugan*
Y–39 Gold and the Dollar Crisis *by Robert Triffin*
Y–40 The Strategy of Economic Development *by Albert O. Hirschman*
Y–41 The Lonely Crowd *by David Riesman*
Y–42 Life of the Past *by George Gaylord Simpson*
Y–43 A History of Russia *by George Vernadsky*
Y–44 The Colonial Background of the American Revolution *by Charles M. Andrews*
Y–45 The Family of God *by W. Lloyd Warner*
Y–46 The Making of the Middle Ages *by R. W. Southern*
Y–47 The Dynamics of Culture Change *by Bronislaw Malinowski*
Y–48 Elementary Particles *by Enrico Fermi*
Y–49 Sweden: The Middle Way *by Marquis W. Childs*
Y–50 Jonathan Dickinson's Journal *edited by Evangeline Walker Andrews and Charles McLean Andrews*
Y–51 Modern French Theatre *by Jacques Guicharnaud*
Y–52 An Essay on Man *by Ernst Cassirer*
Y–53 The Framing of the Constitution of the United States *by Max Farrand*
Y–54 Journey to America *by Alexis de Tocqueville*
Y–55 The Higher Learning in America *by Robert M. Hutchins*
Y–56 The Vision of Tragedy *by Richard B. Sewall*
Y–57 My Eyes Have a Cold Nose *by Hector Chevigny*
Y–58 Child Training and Personality *by John W. M. Whiting and Irvin L. Child*
Y–59 Receptors and Sensory Perception *by Ragnar Granit*
Y–60 Views of Jeopardy *by Jack Gilbert*
Y–61 Long Day's Journey into Night *by Eugene O'Neill*
Y–62 Jay's Treaty *by Samuel Flagg Bemis*
Y–63 Shakespeare: A Biographical Handbook *by Gerald Eades Bentley*
Y–64 The Poetry of Meditation *by Louis L. Martz*
Y–65 Social Learning and Imitation *by Neal E. Miller and John Dollard*
Y–66 Lincoln and His Party in the Secession Crisis *by David M. Potter*

Y-67 SCIENCE SINCE BABYLON *by Derek J. de Solla Price*
Y-68 PLANNING FOR FREEDOM *by Eugene V. Rostow*
Y-69 BUREAUCRACY *by Ludwig von Mises*
Y-70 JOSIAH WILLARD GIBBS *by Lynde Phelps Wheeler*
Y-71 HOW TO BE FIT *by Robert Kiphuth*
Y-72 YANKEE CITY *by W. Lloyd Warner*
Y-73 WHO GOVERNS? *by Robert A. Dahl*
Y-74 THE SOVEREIGN PREROGATIVE *by Eugene V. Rostow*
Y-75 THE PSYCHOLOGY OF C. G. JUNG *by Jolande Jacobi*
Y-76 COMMUNICATION AND PERSUASION *by Carl I. Hovland, Irving L. Janis, and Harold H. Kelley*
Y-77 IDEOLOGICAL DIFFERENCES AND WORLD ORDER *edited by F. S. C. Northrop*
Y-78 THE ECONOMICS OF LABOR *by E. H. Phelps Brown*
Y-79 FOREIGN TRADE AND THE NATIONAL ECONOMY *by Charles P. Kindleberger*
Y-80 VOLPONE *edited by Alvin B. Kernan*
Y-81 TWO EARLY TUDOR LIVES *edited by Richard S. Sylvester and Davis P. Harding*
Y-82 DIMENSIONAL ANALYSIS *by P. W. Bridgman*
Y-83 ORIENTAL DESPOTISM *by Karl A. Wittfogel*
Y-84 THE COMPUTER AND THE BRAIN *by John von Neumann*
Y-85 MANHATTAN PASTURES *by Sandra Hochman*
Y-86 CONCEPTS OF CRITICISM *by René Wellek*
Y-87 THE HIDDEN GOD *by Cleanth Brooks*
Y-88 THE GROWTH OF THE LAW *by Benjamin N. Cardozo*
Y-89 THE DEVELOPMENT OF CONSTITUTIONAL GUARANTEES OF LIBERTY *by Roscoe Pound*
Y-90 POWER AND SOCIETY *by Harold D. Lasswell and Abraham Kaplan*
Y-91 JOYCE AND AQUINAS *by William T. Noon, S.J.*
Y-92 HENRY ADAMS: SCIENTIFIC HISTORIAN *by William Jordy*
Y-93 THE PROSE STYLE OF SAMUEL JOHNSON *by William K. Wimsatt, Jr.*
Y-94 BEYOND THE WELFARE STATE *by Gunnar Myrdal*
Y-95 THE POEMS OF EDWARD TAYLOR *edited by Donald E. Stanford*
Y-96 ORTEGA Y GASSET *by José Ferrater Mora*
Y-97 NAPOLEON: FOR AND AGAINST *by Pieter Geyl*
Y-98 THE MEANING OF GOD IN HUMAN EXPERIENCE *by William Ernest Hocking*
Y-99 THE VICTORIAN FRAME OF MIND *by Walter E. Houghton*
Y-100 POLITICS, PERSONALITY, AND NATION BUILDING *by Lucian W. Pye*

Y-101 MORE STATELY MANSIONS *by Eugene O'Neill*
Y-102 MODERN DEMOCRACY *by Carl L. Becker*
Y-103 THE AMERICAN FEDERAL EXECUTIVE *by W. Lloyd Warner, Paul P. Van Riper, Norman H. Martin, Orvis F. Collins*
Y-104 POEMS 2 *by Alan Dugan*
Y-105 OPEN VISTAS *by Henry Margenau*
Y-106 BARTHOLOMEW FAIR *edited by Eugene M. Waith*
Y-107 LECTURES ON MODERN IDEALISM *by Josiah Royce*
Y-108 SHAKESPEARE'S STAGE *by A. M. Nagler*
Y-109 THE DIVINE RELATIVITY *by Charles Hartshorne*
Y-110 BEHAVIOR THEORY AND CONDITIONING *by Kenneth W. Spence*
Y-111 THE BREAKING OF THE DAY *by Peter Davison*
Y-112 THE GROWTH OF SCIENTIFIC IDEAS *by W. P. D. Wightman*
Y-113 THE PASTORAL ART OF ROBERT FROST *by John F. Lynen*
Y-114 STATE AND LAW: SOVIET AND YUGOSLAV THEORY *by Ivo Lapenna*
Y-115 FUNDAMENTAL LEGAL CONCEPTIONS *by Wesley Newcomb Hohfeld*

THE YALE WESTERN AMERICANA PAPERBOUNDS

YW-1 TRAIL TO CALIFORNIA *edited by David M. Potter*
YW-2 BY CHEYENNE CAMPFIRES *by George Bird Grinnell*
YW-3 DOWN THE SANTA FE TRAIL AND INTO MEXICO *by Susan Shelby Magoffin*
YW-4 A CANYON VOYAGE *by Frederick S. Dellenbaugh*
YW-5 AN INTRODUCTION TO THE STUDY OF SOUTHWESTERN ARCHAEOLOGY *by Alfred Vincent Kidder*
YW-6 THE FUR TRADE IN CANADA *by Harold A. Innis*
YW-7 THE TRUTH ABOUT GERONIMO *by Britton Davis*
YW-8 SUN CHIEF *edited by Leo W. Simmons*
YW-9 SIX YEARS WITH THE TEXAS RANGERS *by James B. Gillett*
YW-10 THE CRUISE OF THE PORTSMOUTH, 1845–1847 *by Joseph T. Downey*